Rw 5/87

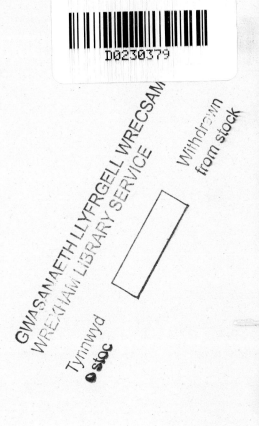

# THE NOVELS OF I. COMPTON-BURNETT

*Photo Cecil Beaton, reproduced by courtesy of Vogue*

# THE NOVELS
# OF I. COMPTON-BURNETT

by

## ROBERT LIDDELL

LONDON
VICTOR GOLLANCZ LTD
1955

Printed in Great Britain by
The Camelot Press Ltd., London and Southampton

# Contents

7

# Introduction

THESE PAGES, prolegomena to the study of a great writer who is happily still alive and writing, necessarily lack finality: a new work of hers may at any time alter the balance of critical appraisement due to her existing novels, and only time can settle her place in the history of English prose fiction. Yet though these pages lack finality they do not necessarily lack justification. A writer ought to be read by his own contemporaries and not wait for posterity; indeed, a writer whose work has not been read in his life-time has very little hope of reaching posterity. A critic is therefore entitled to try to help people to read a living writer, and in this case help is sometimes needed: I have seen in print a sufficient number of errors about Miss Compton-Burnett's work to be convinced that it is not always read as it should be and to fear that it is not often so read. Moreover, one who has owed a great deal to a writer will not gladly withhold his tribute: he would like the satisfaction of expressing gratitude to a living person and to make sure of uttering his testimony before his own death. In the case of the great writers of the past, we are anxious to learn what their contemporaries have said of them: surely it is right to save our literary generation from the discredit of not having issued one book about the novels of Ivy Compton-Burnett.

The serious and even tragic aspects of her art will be considered at some length because many people see her only as a humorous writer. A reviewer some years ago announced his conversion to what he called the cult of Miss Compton-Burnett and declared himself ready to take (so he expressed himself) the sacraments of that mystery religion. Yet shortly afterwards I heard him utter the following heresy in conversation: her novels were extremely amusing, he said, but he did not think they were about Life. There can be very good novels that are not about Life: Peacock's, perhaps, are not about it, and Ronald Firbank's certainly are not. But to read Miss Compton-Burnett is to gain in human experience, and I happen to know that I am not the only reader from whom she has drawn tears.

Great comic writer she obviously is. One of her clowns, a silly, snobbish, pretentious little woman, is allowed to utter a great truth. "I am such a votary of the comic muses. 'No,' I have said, when people have challenged me. 'I will not have comedy pushed into a back place.' I think tragedy and comedy are a greater, wider thing than tragedy by itself. And comedy is so often seen to have tragedy behind it."

She humorously or ironically exploits situations and makes a brilliant use of wit in dialogue: but she is also a great creator of comic characters, characters which ought forever to place her in the central tradition of the English novel and to stop people talking nonsense about the "cult" of Miss Compton-Burnett or the sacraments of her mystery religion. Her toadies, bores and busybodies are splendid creations, full of individuality and life. This scene from *Pastors and Masters* illustrates a single and delightful form of comedy which she has used sparingly in her later work: several absurd characters are seen in action together. The author's detached irony is only allowed the lightest play.

" 'Mrs Merry,' Miss Basden said, in a rather high monotone, 'the boys are saying that the marmalade is watery. I am telling them that no water is used in marmalade, that marmalade does not contain water, so I do not see how it can be.'

" 'I do not see how it can be, either; but of course I wish to be told if anything is not so nice as it can be. Let me taste the marmalade.'

"Miss Basden offered a spoon from the pot.

" 'It seems to me that it is very nice. Perhaps I am not a judge of marmalade. I do not care to eat it on bread with butter myself. One or the other is enough for me. But it seems to be very nice.'

" 'Mother, don't water the boys' preserves,' said Mr Merry, nodding his head up and down. 'Don't try to make things go further than they will go, you know. The game isn't worth the candle.'

" 'I do not understand you, dear. There is never any extra water in preserves. They would not keep if they had water in them. There would not be any object in it. It would be less economical, not more.'

" 'Oh, well, Mother, I don't know anything about the kitchen business and that. But if the marmalade is not right, let us have it right another time. That is all I mean.'

" 'I do not think you know what you mean, dear.'

" 'No, Mother, no; very likely I don't.'

" 'The housekeeping is not your province, Mr Merry,' said

Miss Basden. 'You will have us coming and telling you how to teach Latin if you are not careful.'

" 'Ah, Miss Basden, ah, you saucy lady!' "

In the later books the superb servants'-hall scenes more subtly exhibit this kind of comedy, for they are also commentary and chorus to the scenes of life above-stairs.

There is another element in the later books which should be mentioned here, for the essay that follows is deliberately schematic and only incidentally comments on progress and development in Miss Compton-Burnett's work. As well as a prevailing atmosphere of pity, we feel a sense of the briefness of life and of the approach of death—this writer, always sceptical, watches death approach with a pagan's melancholy.

A brother and sister in *The Present and the Past* contemplate death and annihilation:

" 'You don't think you and I will have an eternity together?'

" 'No, but we shall have until we are seventy. And there is no difference.'

" 'Can you bear not to have the real thing?'

" 'No,' said his sister.

" 'Then when you are older, will you begin to have beliefs?'

" 'No, I shall realize the hopelessness of things. I shall meet it face to face.'

" 'And will you be proud of doing that?'

" 'Well, think how few people can do it. And I must have some compensation; it will not be much.'

" 'I shall not be able to face it. I shall begin to say we cannot be quite sure.'

" 'And I shall like to hear you say it. Even a spurious comfort is better than nothing.' "

The brother and sister are still young—there is a more poignant conversation in *Darkness and Day* between Gaunt Lovat and his old friend, Sir Ransom Chace, who is on his deathbed.

" 'You will leave a great blank. I shall never find things quite the same.'

" 'But you will find them nearly the same? Life will not be over for you?'

" 'I do not believe in not taking people on equal terms until the end. Your mind is not failing. You are as much a man as I am. You would know if I distorted the truth.'

" 'Truth is so impossible. Something has to be done with it. If you had said you would find life quite different, I should have believed it. I think I do believe it.'

" 'I think I do too,' said Gaunt, in another tone. 'I shall be a lonely man when you are gone.' "

A comic writer often loses the credit for realizing "the hopelessness of things" and for knowing that "truth is so impossible." It is not surprising that Miss Compton-Burnett has been ignored or passed over with a slighting reference by that school of critics who, for all their discernment, have made the mistake of finding Congreve shallow and heartless; their initial mistake has perhaps been due to the fact that, with their imperfect sense of humour, they have not been able to find either of them really comic.

There are some authors, and she is one, who, in addition to their outer circle of readers and admirers, have also an inner circle to whom they seem to speak more intimately. There are people whose special author Miss Compton-Burnett is—to us, her work is no private religion or snobbery—it is a source of intense and peculiar intellectual excitement and pleasure. It is also one of the things we live by: a standard for our own conduct (in spite of our shortcomings and backslidings) and a support in bad times.

# CHAPTER 1

## *The Beginning*

---

THE AUTHOR'S LITERARY history has been strange; before her serious work began with *Pastors and Masters* (1925) there were fourteen years of silence. In 1911, as a young woman, she had published *Dolores*; one cannot imagine her giving such a name to any of her later books or characters.

*Dolores* is regarded by Miss Compton-Burnett as a juvenile work and perhaps she would prefer to forget it. It should not be read, for it is misleading, by anyone who does not thoroughly know and care for the work of her maturity. Nevertheless, for the critic, it has great interest.

The style, more narrative than dialogue, is markedly different from that of the later books; never again shall we find sentimentality or the language of Wardour Street. It is an ungainly style, which I have elsewhere described as "crude, bare, and rather alarming. It is not real English: it is like the language of translation. It reminds one of English translations of Russian novels and of Greek tragedy, and one may conjecture that both of them had formed an important part of her reading. Such a style is un-euphonious and harsh, but conscientiously renders a meaning—and that is what, like a translator, Miss Compton-Burnett already did, with a remarkable exactitude."[1]

The precision of this early style has been, as we shall see, extraordinarily refined in her later work, though she has never

[1] *A Treatise on the Novel* (Cape, 1947), p. 149.

seemed to care very much about euphony. Such an exact but ugly sentence as: "He is certainly different to me from to them", which occurs in *Dolores*, is to be found, almost unchanged, in very much later and more mature work. Nor has the woodenness of much of the dialogue in this book entirely disappeared from her other novels.

Nevertheless, the wit shines out in the speeches of the two village bores, Mr Blackwood and Dr Cassell, though the writer has not yet acquired enough art to create a bore who is felt as boring the other characters but never bores the reader. There is, however, a new note in the dialogue; it would be much to expect a critic in 1911 to have heard it, but to those who know her later work it is clearly discernible. It is a remarkable thing that the author has thrown away everything in *Dolores* which was not worth keeping, and has developed the strong point that she already displayed there. Her gift for epigram is also shown; epigram that is not merely "smart" but that sums up a great deal of knowledge of life.

"He happened to be an exception to the rule that enthusiasm for religious subjects is coupled with a tendency to pleasantry upon them."

"The disposition to talk for the display of information had grown—though it happened that the information had not sustained a similar process."

The almost classical unity of place and action of the later

books is not here found; the action takes place in a Yorkshire village, in a women's college in Oxford, and in the house of a dramatist living in the same city.

But the main difference in this work from that of the author's maturity lies in the moral values. Dolores, on at least seven occasions, immolates herself for people who are not worth her sacrifice, and we are expected to regard her self-sacrifice as noble: in the later books such self-sacrifice would be regarded as horrible, destructive both of the persons by and for whom it was made.

First she gives up an academic career to undertake the education of her young half-brother and half-sisters; then she gives up home life again to avoid friction with her stepmother, when the education of these children is otherwise provided for; in Oxford she again makes a place for herself and is able to be of real use to a great writer in his work, but she abandons both because her stepmother dies and her father calls her home. She hands over two very superior men, for either of whom she would have been the ideal wife and companion, one to a college friend, and the other to a young half-sister. She refuses to act as assistant to the great dramatist, now growing blind, during his last months of life because she believes her father has the first claim on her time. When her father makes a third marriage, she again leaves home and returns to an academic career.

# CHAPTER 2

## *The Tyrants*

THERE IS A VERY terrible passage in Amiel's *Journal* where, in a page, he sums up what is the main subject of Miss Compton-Burnett's novels.

"Oh, the Family! If the superstition with which loyalty and religion have surrounded that institution would allow the truth to be told, to what account would it not be called! What an innumerable company of martyrs it has sullenly, inexorably, forced into submission! What hearts it has stifled, lacerated, broken! What oubliettes, what death-sentences, what dungeons, what abominable tortures in its annals, darker than those of the Spanish Inquisition. One could fill all the wells of the earth with the tears it has caused to be shed in secret, one could people a planet with the beings it has made wretched, could double the average of human life with the years of those whose days it has shortened. Oh, the suspicions, the jealousies, the rancours, the hates of the family, who has measured their depth? And the venomous words, the insults that never cease to rankle, the invisible thrusts of the stiletto, the infernal second intentions in speech, for that matter the mere irreparable slips of the tongue, the deadly chattering, what a legion of suffering have they not engendered."

Words such as these of Amiel are apt to seem hysterical

to people who have been happy at home. Some people are always loath to believe atrocity stories and it is pity as well as complacency that is the motive of their disbelief. "People are not so wicked as all that" is the good-natured and common-sense reaction to stories of life under the Spanish Inquisition, in German or Japanese concentration camps, in Russia or Jugoslavia; refugees in all times and from all places have had a tendency to whine.

Refugees from family life often whine, and some of their stories are exaggerated. Morover, the family, unlike Inquisition, Gestapo, Ogpu or Osna, is rooted in human nature: some, at least, of its misfits are likely to be in the wrong.

Nevertheless, there are plenty of well-attested atrocity stories of family lives where isolation, idiosyncrasy and unchecked powers have been terribly productive of evil and of the helpless suffering of the innocent. The biographies of a few men and women of genius have enabled us to look into some very dark and strange places: the dramatic and tragic parsonage at Haworth; the even more sinister Lincolnshire parsonage where the "black" Tennysons lived; the parsonage, more smugly evil, where Samuel Butler passed his boyhood; the house in Wimpole Street, from which Elizabeth Barrett escaped to marry Robert Browning; the wicked home on Denmark Hill, from which Effie Ruskin was goaded into flight.

We know about these evil homes because of the genius and the courage of some of their inmates. There are many others that have left no memorial—though sometimes the *faits divers* in the newspapers, our own experience or horrifying glimpses into other lives, add more modern instances.

The nineteenth century in England—the age of the Tennysons, Brontës, Butlers, Barretts and Ruskins—was the great age of unhappy families. It was also the age of Constance Kent, an unhinged adolescent—as much a Compton-Burnett character as old Mr Barrett, that incestuous tyrant, or vile old Mrs Ruskin—who murdered her baby half-brother out of spite against her stepmother. It was an age, too, when family dissensions and jealousies so raged among the Tichbornes that a butcher from Wapping was able to pass himself off among many people as the heir of that old Catholic family.

Jane Austen's had been, in this respect, a gentler age. The theme of family tyranny crops out, indeed, in her treatment of Mrs Norris or of General Tilney. But in her time the human family was still an organic and natural thing, directed, like the family in the animal world, towards the rearing of the young. The young were encouraged to start on independent lines of their own as soon as possible, and the marrying-off of daughters was not so much an exercise of parental authority as a release of the daughters from that authority—like rooks throwing their young out of the nest to teach them to fly.

On the whole, in Jane Austen's novels, the relations between adult men and women and their parents are those of friendship, even of warm affection; parents as cold and callous as Sir Walter Elliot or Mrs Ferrars are in a minority. There is little sign of the emotional love or hatred, none of the religious awe that we find in Victorian memoirs or fiction.

It was the growing prosperity of the middle classes which had made parents in less of a hurry to get rid of their children. The young remained longer at home before marriage and the parents (having themselves often made late marriages) were more distant in age from the younger generation than eighteenth-century parents had generally been. The religious revivals had made people more familiar with the Bible, in particular with the Old Testament: Victorians were prone to bring Hebraic standards into their private lives. The sacrifice of Abraham's son or of Jephthah's daughter entered into their imaginations and their talk, as did the obedience of the descendants of Jonadab the son of Rechab. A later development was the cult of childhood—which came to be thought a beautiful state and one worthy of prolongation, instead of a necessary phase that must be gone through before maturity is reached and had better be gone through as quickly as possible.

On the whole, family life is now less formidable than it was in the nineteenth century: poverty, women's freedom and the decline of religion have all contributed to this end. Daughters and sons both go early to work, often far from their homes, and the Bible is little read—perhaps the neglect of the New Testament is made up for by the decreased influence of the Old. Above all, parents are less isolated from other people and have less leisure for making parenthood a whole-time occupation.

On this change Miss Burnett's *Conversation* with Miss Margaret Jourdain provides a comment.

"Isolation and leisure," Miss Jourdain had said, "seem necessary for the rearing of strange family growths."

"Isolation and leisure," Miss Compton-Burnett replied, "put nothing into people. But they give what is there full play. They allow it to grow according to itself, and this may be strongly in certain directions.

"I am sure that the people who were middle-aged and elderly when I was young were more individualized than are now my own contemporaries. The effect of wider intercourse and self-adaptation seems to go below the surface and the result is that the essence of people is controlled and modified.

The people may be better and do less harm, but they afford less interest as a study. This is surely the real meaning of the saying that personalities belong to the past.

"Imagine a Winston Churchill, untaught and untrained and adapted in the sense we mean, and then immured in an isolated life in a narrow community, and think what might have happened to his power, what would have happened to it."

That is the sort of thing Miss Compton-Burnett has imagined. She looks further than Gray and sees that although a country churchyard may now hold

Some Cromwell, guiltless of his country's blood

he will certainly have been guilty of other things.

"I think," she says, "that life makes great demand on people's characters, and gives them, and especially used to give them, great opportunity to serve their own ends by the sacrifice of other people. Such ill-doing may meet with little retribution, may indeed be hardly recognized, and I cannot feel so surprised if people yield to it."

While many novelists in the present age might have written to illustrate the theories of Freud, Miss Compton-Burnett has not interested herself in sexual passion: its consequences, as they affect family life, are deeply interesting to her—we find marriage, adultery and incest taking place, and homosexuality implied—but she lacks Jane Austen's interest in passion. It would be rash to say that she could not portray it if she chose —the troubled youth of Grant Edgeworth in *A House and Its Head*, the young love of Gabriel and Ruth in *More Women Than Men*, suggest that she has gifts which she has not yet chosen to use to the full. It is the lust for power that she so penetratingly examines.

22

Miss Compton-Burnett has dated her novels between 1885 and 1901—with the exception of the sketch, *Pastors and Masters*, where the events must have taken place later than 1918. One or two of the books are given no precise date, though the action evidently takes place at the end of the nineteenth century. She has chosen the end of the age of isolation and leisure and, though we may feel that this was the last age in which we would have chosen to live, she shows us that it was the one age really propitious for the rearing of the strange family growths in which she delights. Perhaps it was not altogether a free choice on her part. It is natural for an artist to revert to the age of his own childhood, and she has written: "I do not feel that I have any real or organic knowledge of life later than about 1910. I should not write of later times with enough grasp or confidence. I think this is why many writers tend to write of the past. When an age is ended, you see it as it is."

This does not at all mean that her novels are "dated"—their action is set in a period when family life could be lived and studied in isolation better than it can at present, when the impact of public life is often so close and so cruel. But her facts are eternal: every year still adds abominable tortures to the annals of the Family, even if they are fewer, and this will go on until the consummation of time. Her theme is older than literature—Euripides has been credited with the invention of Love, but no one has suggested that Aeschylus or Sophocles invented Unhappy Families: they existed before Agamemnon.

"Oh, the suspicions, the jealousies, the rancours, the hates of the family, who has measured their depth?" Amiel uttered his cry in 1868. Seventy years later his question could have been answered: Miss Compton-Burnett has measured them.

In her last three novels, Miss Compton-Burnett has no central figure of a tyrant; the families in these books are not deeply unhappy, the tedium and wanhope of their lives spring from the family atmosphere and are due to the oppressiveness of love rather than to anyone's wickedness.

In her early novel *Dolores* (published in 1911), the father, Cleveland Hutton, is hardly seen as a tyrant. His selfish claims on his daughter, Dolores, are always liable to break up the academic career she has made for herself, and he is not un-critically viewed. But the daughter's sacrifice is, in this im-mature book, seen as noble—almost in the spirit in which Tennyson saw that of Jephthah's daughter or of Iphigenia. With her mature mind the author sees such sacrifices as horrible, and this youthful work (interesting for the seeds of further development which can be discerned in it) must be regarded as outside the canon of her work.

The first ten novels of her maturity contain a wonderful portrait gallery of family tyrants. Three of them are fathers—and Henry Bentley, in *Pastors and Masters*, has an additional sanction given to his power by his position as a clergyman. Another tyrant is a grandfather, believing that his patriarchal position gives him divine right over his descendants. On the whole, the male tyrants are quite honestly despotic—they believe that their absolute rule is beneficial to those who suffer it; and in one respect they have no illusion about them-selves—they know that they are despots.

The male tyrants are all country gentlemen living on in-herited property which they have done nothing to augment; nevertheless they resent in the young their unproductiveness (a natural consequence of youth and of lack of opportunity), they afford only grudging support to the creatures whom they have brought into the world; yet they expect, and sometimes even demand, gratitude.

They are alike in position and the sameness of their position often involves them in similar episodes; they have the stylized speech of all Miss Compton-Burnett's characters. Like them all, it is in *character* that they differ.

Henry Bentley belongs to what Henry James would have called the "treatment" rather than the "subject" of *Pastors and Masters*. He is not fully developed, but in the few pages devoted to him we have a very promising first draft of a tyrant. With the basic characteristics of the male tyrant he combines a neurotic and self-dramatizing power of nagging that is more often given to the female of the species.

" 'You see, John, it is not always an easy thing to bring people to see what is right, when one is at the head of a household where people are fond of having their own way, whether it is the right way or not. It cannot be done, my boy, without much of what must seem to people who do not understand—and my family are people who do not understand, I am sorry to say—to be needless, and even trying. But you will look back upon what your father did, when I am no longer with you, and see that it was not done easily.'

"John looked at his father with rising tears.

"Mr Bentley just laid a hand on his head, and went upstairs and stood by himself, repeating his speech with additions which had not occurred to him."

Duncan Edgeworth, in *A House and Its Head,* is a completely male tyrant. Like all the more developed tyrants he is not a mere monster of egoism: he has some of the qualities of his defects, notably probity and moral strength. He is not without generosity. Other men like him; and a woman of the highest integrity, who has lived in his house as his daughters' governess, is willing to become his third wife.

" 'He behaved like a god,' said one of his daughters, 'and we simply treated him as one. It shows what it is, never to have any criticism. Gods contrive to have nothing but praise; they definitely arrange it; it is true they are all wise.' "

The god whom Duncan resembled was Jehovah, and the imitation may not have been wholly unconscious. The tyrannical grandfather in *Parents and Children*, Sir Jesse Sullivan, was more like a pagan god; his position was not much shaken when it was found that he had a family of illegitimate children. He believed in his divine right to govern his family and exercised this right unjustly and capriciously, as if he were Jupiter. Like Jupiter he was further away from mere humanity than Jehovah, and his wrath and his loving-kindness were less immediate and less unwholesome than Duncan's in their impact.

The third tyrannical father, Horace Lamb, is the most evil male tyrant; he combines miserliness with despotism.

"You crushed the spring of childhood, bound it with constraint and fear, forced it to deception and visited the wrong you caused"—so his wife told him. He is the only male tyrant forced by events to a realization of what he has done and is unique in making a real attempt to reform—though it is self-interested and doomed to failure.

Of the female tyrants, Sabine Ponsonby, the grandmother in *Daughters and Sons*, is also frank about her despotism: she was born in an earlier and more honest age and is as downright as a man. The two tyrannical mothers are deadlier and exercise a more subtle sway. They wish to rule by love (and indeed they inspire love); it is not enough for them to drive their subjects —they also wish to lead them. It is, however, very much better to be driven rather than led by a tyrant: your inner liberty is safe and you can call your soul your own. It is a pity that schoolmasters like writing, and parents seem to like reading, on a report that a child "can be led and not driven"— probably this is one of the sentimental fabrications due to the public-school spirit. After all, we can all be driven, and one would rather admire a child who could not be led. I have also heard of a child described as "disobedient but loyal"—and I hope and believe that I was just the opposite myself, as are all Miss Compton-Burnett's good, young characters.

The first of the tyrannical mothers, Sophia Stace, tries to claim a superior sensitiveness to that of other people. She is indeed a sensitive woman, and on one occasion uses her powers of perception very finely to help two young relations through an intolerable moment of crisis.


" 'Sophia, I couldn't have done it better if I had rehearsed it for a week,' said Christian.

" 'Ah, you will never get to the end of finding what I can do,' said Sophia with a flash of her eyes. 'You will always go on discovering that. I sometimes find myself marvelling at the gulf between the average person and myself.' "


She tries to widen this gulf by working up her own feelings and by exhausting the feelings of others through her excessive demands upon them. Unlike Harriet Haslam, the other tyrant mother, she is a wife first and a mother afterwards—deeply in love with her husband and avenging his illness and death upon her children, who feel them, indeed, but cannot in nature feel them as deeply or in the same way as she does.

Harriet Haslam, in *Men and Wives*, has two claims to power: high idealism, and nervous sickness. Miss Hansford-Johnson,[1] extraordinarily, calls her a "comic monster", and, no less extraordinarily, says that we never see her as she appears to herself or to other people unaffected by her "atrocious selfishness".

In fact, Harriet (apart from Sukey Donne in *Elders and Betters*) is the only female tyrant who ever doubts her own righteousness.

In the terrible speech in which she asks her doctor for the means of suicide, Harriet gives a true account of herself:

" 'I see my children's faces, and am urged by the hurt of them to go further, and driven on to the worst. I retrace my way in my mind, trying to grasp at what they remember; I almost overtake it and it goes; and each time I reach it less and less, until I hope to get only to a certain point and then less far; and my brain is numb. . . .

" 'And it must happen again. They are young, and are planning their lives for themselves in the way of the young. They need forbearance even from those who have strength for it, and I have no strength. I feel anything less than perfection would break down my brain. And my poor ones do

---

[1] In her pamphlet on this author, published for the British Council and the National Book League (London, 1951).

not reach it—how should they, being children of mine?—and the round begins. And the night comes again.' "

Harriet is a tragic figure, and there are people outside her household who love and admire her uprightness and the graciousness of which she is capable: Antony Dufferin, her doctor, and Rachel Hardisty, her best friend, are people of integrity who are not in the least blind to her dreadful faults; even poor, snobbish Mrs Christy, who toadies to her, has a genuine feeling for her. Moreover, though Harriet wants to interfere with her children's lives unwarrantably, she really does know what is best for them.

The tyrannical aunts are, on the whole, the most evil of all. Sukey Donne, one of the two invalids reigning from their sofas, is the exception: she has a great deal of charm and distinction and she has Harriet's power of self-criticism, for she can say of a mean act of her own: "I wanted my revenge for the little neglects, that loom so large to a sick mind." She is only half-heartedly a tyrant, and in her case the concessions that are made to a sick person are really her due; she proves the genuineness of her sickness by dying of it.

The other three aunts are whole-heartedly tyrants. Josephine Napier, who combines the function of very efficient head-mistress with that of aunt, has for her weapons charm and the service of others more than those others require. Her essential dishonesty is indicated in a small scene at the beginning of the book.

" 'You are very kind, Mrs Napier.'

" 'No. Why am I kind?' said Josephine, seeming to speak in an aside from jotting something down. 'You have always done all you can for me.'

" 'I will certainly do it, Mrs Napier,' said Miss Rosetti, her eyes just resting on Josephine's empty page, as she left the room."

Josephine is unfaithful in great things as well as in little things, and is the only tyrant who commits murder. She is continually showing off, and she acts so well the part of considerate employer and careful guardian of the young that she does much real kindness. One would as soon send a child to her school as to any other in fiction. She is also the kind of woman who needs to have a man emotionally dependent on her, and she boasts of her nephew Gabriel's devotion to an extent that is almost indecent. These boasts become untruthful and almost pathetic as the young man begins to transfer his devotion to a girl of nearer his own age.

Hetta Ponsonby in *Daughters and Sons* is as possessive as Josephine; her brother John, a widower, is the victim of her excessive devotion—and she boasts with the same pathetic fallaciousness, the same forgeries of jealousy, as her power wanes. But hers is a very different personality and she totally lacks Josephine's charm. Her position in the family is also very different—under the old grandmother, she acts as assistant-tyrant over a motherless household: "she was an influence at once dubious and powerful, at once natural and sinister, an authority at once lower and higher than Sabine". Miss Rosetti, a clear-sighted woman who knows the very worst about Josephine, still loves her. Hetta is the most unfortunate of tyrants, for nearly every character in the book knows the worst about her and no one but her mother loves her.

Matilda Seaton, the terrible Aunt Matty of *A Family and a Fortune*, is the wickedest of all the domestic tyrants. Her power is purely moral and not at all economic—Hetta Ponsonby and Sukey Donne at least contributed to the household expenses, and the latter engaged in the nineteenth-century sport of will-shaking; all the other tyrants controlled the purse-strings. Matty, however, was like Mrs Norris in *Mansfield Park*, a comparatively poor relation, dependent for extra comforts upon the family in the big house which she tyrannized over from her little house at its gates.

She claimed the privileges of an invalid but with less excuse than Sukey Donne. "A fall from a horse had rendered her an invalid, or rather obliged her to walk with a stick." Sophia Stace, also, had had a hunting fall, but it only resulted in a "sidelong movement".

Her boastfulness, unlike Josephine's, is about the unverifiable past.


" 'Yes, I was a naughty, sprightly person . . . Always looking for something on which to work my wits. Something or someone; I fear it did not matter as long as my penetration had its exercise. Well, we can't choose the pattern on which we are made. And perhaps I would not alter mine. Perhaps there is no need to meddle with it. . . .

" 'Yes, there are stories waiting for you of Aunt Matty in her heyday, when the world was young, or seemed to keep itself young for her, as things did somehow adapt themselves to her in those days.' "

Her particular form of wickedness is putting people in the wrong. "She attributes motives to people, whether they are there or not," says one of her nephews. But cruel though she is to her sister's family, from whom she takes a great deal of kindness, her worst cruelty is reserved for her paid companion, Miss Griffin.

In one of those terrible scenes, she is like a viler Mrs Norris after the day at Sotherton.

" 'That is to be the result of a little change and pleasure. I must see that you do not have it. I see that it does not work. I must take counsel with myself and arrange for your life to be nothing but duty, as that is what seems to suit you.' "

There are worse scenes than this; at the end of one of the most brutal, they are interrupted by a call from Dudley Gaveston, who has come to tell Matty that her friend, Maria Sloane, formerly engaged to himself, has transferred her affections to his elder brother.

Matty rises to the demands of the occasion—like Josephine Napier or Sophia Stace she is a sensitive woman and has great powers of intelligent sympathy; if she were not able to put herself in other people's places, she would not be capable of being so nasty.

" 'Well, so I am to hear what has happened, all of it from the beginning. You tell me, Dudley. You are too interested in the whole panorama of life to be biased by your own little share.

You know that I use the word, little, in its relation to your mind, not to mine. So tell me about it, and when it is all to take place. . . . You won't think there is anything I do not want to hear. I include all human experience in my range. You and I are at one there.'

" 'I think you have got me over my first moment better than anyone,' said Dudley. . . ."

A later moment in the same conversation is also significant:

" 'I am sure you would not dare to˜pity me,' [said Dudley]. 'If you would, I must just face the hardest part.'

" 'Well, you know, I do not feel that about pity. I often feel that I deserve it and do not get my share. People so soon forget to give it.'

" 'That is another kind thing to say. But is pity really better than forgetfulness? Then I still have to suffer the worst indeed.' "

Matty is also generous to Maria, who finds herself in an ungracious position; and at the end of the book, in Dudley's illness, she is selfless in her help to the family that she has persecuted. But she is the one tyrant whose rage, bitterness and malice are continually unveiled and uncontrolled.

This is the part of the family portrait gallery devoted to the tyrants and it is by no means a Chamber of Horrors; powerful for evil, the tyrants are also powerful for good, and most of them use their powers in this direction also. Henry Bentley is only a faint sketch; of the fully drawn tyrants, it is only Hetta Ponsonby who does no good action and speaks no kindly word. Before the story begins, she must have had good actions to her credit, otherwise her present position would not be believable. "She tried to live for others," comments one of her nieces, "and people try to improve what they live for, and that is the end."

The tyrants are more varied and complex beings than critics are often willing to admit. Some readers have also complained that they do not remember or distinguish them after they have closed the books. This is a subjective criticism, to which one can only oppose the experience of a reader who could unerringly assign any speech to the right speaker and for whom all the eleven tyrants remain distinct in the memory.

# CHAPTER 3

## *The Happenings*

---

THE TYRANTS ARE not purely evil; each of them (with two exceptions only) enjoys the friendship of a discerning good character—and Miss Compton-Burnett's good characters are very good indeed. With these two exceptions—Henry Bentley and Hetta Ponsonby—there is no tyrant among them whom the reader must not from time to time admire.

There is therefore no unpleasant feeling that the writer has been working off any sort of grudge. Nearly every novel ends in some kind of reconciliation and pardon, not a sentimental happy ending but a kind of sober calm, like the close of Greek tragedy.

Before this stage is attained, something terrible must happen to clear the air—either there is a violent happening or some old and discreditable secret is brought to light—the two classical processes of the Greek tragedians, *peripeteia* and *anagnorisis*. In one or two books, notably in *A House and Its Head*, both effects are used.

The crimes vary among such peccadilloes as theft, fornication, adultery and incest, suppression of wills, attempted bigamy, infanticide, murder of a niece-by-marriage and matricide. The great distinction of the author is that she can make these happenings credible. Some readers will, of course, believe nothing—but she shows that some of her characters have strong enough motives to commit these crimes and good enough chances of getting away with them. It is not necessarily true that murder will out—these books are far more true to life than detective stories, where people so willingly give information against their friends. In life, and it is much to their credit, people dissemble—even commit perjury in court. Anyone who has ever felt or received any affection can surely imagine himself as an accomplice after the fact. Moreover, if we think for a moment of the skeletons in our own family cupboards and those that we know or guess at in the cupboards of other people, Miss Compton-Burnett's plots do not appear absurd. She loves *peripeteia* for the sake of the revelation of human nature that it brings: but her plots are no "arbitrary framework".

"I think," she says, "there are signs that strange things happen, though they do not emerge. I believe it would go ill with many of us if we were faced with a strong temptation, and I suspect that with some of us it does go ill."

The tension of family life is such that we feel nerves must snap. The dreadful breakfast table scenes, with their "venomous words", "insults that never cease to rankle" and "invisible thrusts of the stiletto", are so pregnant with horror that we should have a sense of anti-climax if nothing happened.

Here are two sinister passages from *Daughters and Sons*.

" 'I see why a portrait of a family group is called a Conversation Piece,' said Rowland, coming to escort Miss Marcon. 'They don't generally have such good names for things.'

" 'Not such dreadful ones. I daren't look at these pictures, because of what I might read into them. It is really too morbid to paint family groups, with a father and mother and children, and no attempt to leave out anything. After all, why dwell on these things? It does not alter them.' "

" 'People believe in the sanctity of the home,' said France. 'It makes them let themselves go. They think that the sanctity is over everything, and it is astonishing how it seems to be.' "

There is no crime in *Dolores*.

In *Pastors and Masters* the author was still trying her hand: her point of view was completely mature, she might have been a hundred years old in experience and wisdom—but in letters she seems still to have been uncertain what she could do. The plot is not integrated and the little crime is nothing to do with the tyranny.

A little crime it is. Richard Bumpus tries to rewrite a work abandoned in his youth, and leaves the manuscript in the room of a dying friend; Nicholas Herrick finds it there after the friend's death, thinks it is the dead man's work and tries to steal it. Miss Hansford-Johnson oddly misstates the happenings, and adds that "Life goes on, rather the worse for wear". In fact, Life is none the worse, though not positively the better.

In *Brothers and Sisters* there is a double *anagnorisis* or revelation. Andrew Stace adopts his own natural son, Christian, keeping him in ignorance of his parentage: when Christian wants to marry Sophia, Andrew's legitimate daughter and his own half-sister, the young people mistake the old man's opposition for motiveless tyranny; he gives them no adequate reason for it and threatens them with disinheritance. "I would not stoop to use absolute power like that. It shows how degrading absolute power can be," says Sophia—an ironical speech from one who is to become a tyrant mother.

Sophia locks up a document, which she fears may be a will disinheriting her and Christian if they marry; it is a letter telling

Christian that they are brother and sister. Twenty-eight years later, in a fit of superstitious remorse, Sophia makes her half-brother, her husband for twenty-seven years, unlock the drawer. The shock gives him a fatal heart attack but the paper gets locked away again—the secret comes out fully during Sophia's last illness; she learns it then for the first time and in her weakness is unable to keep it to herself.

A sub-plot and a lesser discovery prepare the way for the climax. Christian's mother, now a widowed Mrs Lang with a son and daughter, settles in the village where Christian is lord of the manor. She discovers the relationship in time to prevent her son Gilbert from an incestuous marriage with Christian's daughter Dinah, and her daughter Caroline from a like marriage with Christian's son Andrew—their niece and nephew by the half-blood. Then Mrs Lang dies, resolutely silent about Christian's father.

In the village of Moreton Edge, with its five gentle households—the kind of setting in which Jane Austen delighted—the Theban tragedy is re-enacted.

Sophia is directly in the Theban line: when Christian's health is threatened, she thinks it may be due to a curse on the family, incurred when she locked up a document twenty-eight years ago.

Gilbert says: "We are beginning to leave off feeling branded, but all our friends seem shy of us. It is too like an ancient tragedy for them."

Dinah says: ". . . we are apart from our race in the thing at the root of our being. We have always seemed to be something of the kind. Perhaps the truth behind us was working itself out."

Sophocles, one feels, is being given the acknowledgement of his help that is elsewhere given to Jane Austen: and Sophia, like Oedipus, though not willingly guilty of incest is yet not a wholly innocent person. A character in a later book, Anna Donne in *Elders and Betters*, seems to have learned by Sophia's mistake: if you have suppressed a will, it is more prudent to go on suppressing it. Sophia gains a pathos from her unfortunate secret in spite of her tyranny—and after her death the book ends quietly, with some degree of peace and consolation.

Any analysis of the events of *Brothers and Sisters* must make them seem very much more improbable than they appear to the reader of the book; this is not to say that no strain is imposed on his credulity. And the plot is shambling, as well as having an awkward jump of twenty-seven years between the first two chapters.

*Men and Wives* has tyrannicide for its theme—the plot has a classical balance and is perhaps the finest that Miss Compton-Burnett has ever contrived. Harriet Haslam, who has tyrannized over her family, in a moment of despair makes an attempt at suicide: the drug she has taken is harmless, but the shock overturns her mental balance and she goes into a home for treatment. In her absence, her family begin to lead their own lives—she returns, beyond expectation cured, and starts to reassert her old power. A return to the bad old days, after a period of relaxation, is particularly intolerable (the same thing is felt by the victims in *Manservant and Maidservant*). Matthew Haslam procures a drug that is not harmless, and kills his mother.

The murderer, in reaction, confesses his crime: two family friends try to persuade him that he is suffering from a delusion

and succeed in forcing him to accept this as the official explanation. The family is left in a state of willing suspension of
disbelief—the exact shade of which varies with each member;
a thing utterly true to life.

"So the uncredited Oedipus goes away," is Miss Hansford-
Johnson's comment—can she mean Orestes?—"and the
Family, that invulnerable, indestructible unit, ruthless, wilfully
blind and tenacious as death, continues on its appointed road."
In fact, the Haslam family is happier and better; the air is
cleared by the crime and everyone has been purged by the
terror and the pity of it. The strength of the family has been
manifested, not only its weakness—family hatred makes a son
kill his mother (whom he also loves); family love makes his
brothers and sister shield him.

The best plots are those where the tyrant is author or victim
of the crime. In *Manservant and Maidservant*, the mean tyrant,
Horace Lamb, is first the victim of an abortive plot: his wife
Charlotte plans with his cousin Mortimer to leave him, and to
rescue her children from him. He finds out this plot, and
transforms himself into a kind father.

Charlotte's speech to him is eloquent:

" 'Mortimer and I could not suffer the things in this house;
we were at the end of our power to suffer. We could let helpless
children suffer no longer, after seeing them do so all their
lives. We thought of the way of escape for us all, and we were
going to take it. It would have been the right way, and the
only right one. But I have come home to find this difference,
this difference that there might always have been. If you had
been like this always, Horace! If you had lived this life from

the first! This is proof that you could have done so, that you could have made the hard path easy. It does not show the past years in a better light. But for the moment our case is gone. Whether it may return or not is another thing, but for the moment it is gone. The future is in your hands, and you have the power to hold it. But the past is my tragedy and your fault.' "

She adds a warning:

" 'You have those years to live down. The children have those years in their memories, their spoiled childhood in their hearts. Any lapse must come as something added to these.' "

Horace cannot keep up his amendment: there is a lapse and, as his aunt, Emilia, says, it takes on "the guise of a threat too great to be borne". He walks off towards a bridge that has been declared dangerous: he does not know the danger but his sons Marcus and Jasper know—nevertheless they do not stop him. They think of the danger too late—think what a relief his death will be—think it is too late to warn him—and then think they have killed him. The confusion of their thought, the illusion of responsibility is beautifully done. Horace, of course, takes the worst and meanest view of their action, but is met by the beautiful uprightness of the children and the noble wisdom of the nurse, who protects them from their father and from the dangers of a false memory.

The happenings are dramatic but not at all improbable:

probably children contemplate or attempt parricide, matricide and fratricide very much more often than sentimental child-lovers would like to believe. Sometimes they achieve it—are all the "accidental homicides" committed by children really accidental?

Josephine Napier, in *More Women Than Men*, is the great tyrant-murderess: she kills to preserve power, exposing her nephew's young wife to the cold when the girl has pneumonia. This is a method of murder that the Crime Club probably does not think highly of; but what doctor would be willing to swear that none of his patients could have been a victim of it? "There are signs that strange things happen, though they do not emerge."

Josephine suffers no legal retribution for her crime. Her remorse at first is violent but it seems to be short-lived. She would have a short memory for her misdeeds: she is not another Sophia Stace. But she suffers the punishment that commonly comes to the condemned perpetrators of crimes of passion long before they reach the gallows or the electric chair: she no longer wants that for which she has killed. Thus the atmosphere is lightened: Josephine is nicer, less possessive, really better for having killed Ruth. Miss Compton-Burnett evidently does not believe in the superstition that the killer always kills again.

In *Daughters and Sons* the criminal is again a tyrant who is losing power: Hetta Ponsonby pretends to have killed herself and we cannot be quite certain that she did not at one time really intend to do so. Like Harriet, she returns to a household which has learned to do without her—but she has killed her authority for good.

Another pretended attempt at suicide occurs in *The Present and the Past.* This time it is exposed as completely insincere: Cassius Clare deliberately took an insufficient dose of sleeping pills (or whatever the unidentified drug was) to do the work. Cassius, however, is too ineffective to be a tyrant.

The only other tyrant directly involved in a violent happening is Matilda Seaton—but she is not quite in the centre of the picture and the happening is a little less than a crime: she chases her martyred companion, Miss Griffin, into the snow. Later, in a scene of blood-curdling horror, she laughs over the poor woman's plight. Thereafter most of her power is gone; it was already on the wane.

*A House and Its Head* should probably be reckoned among the best plots. Though the tyrannical Duncan Edgeworth is neither criminal nor victim, the crimes result from the oppressive atmosphere that he has generated.

Alison, his second wife, commits incestuous adultery with his nephew Grant, by whom she has a son, recognized as Duncan's and barring Grant's succession to the entailed property. Duncan's daughter Sibyl marries Grant: she is an unbalanced and alarming young woman, of the Constance Kent type. She suborns a dismissed servant to murder her small stepbrother and stepson, Richard, so that her husband may again be heir.

The discovery and the hushing-up of the crime are ingenious —detective fiction would require a little more of each, but this is not detective fiction and the author has done enough for her purpose. No one wishes Sibyl to be convicted but those members of the family who know of it find it understandably hard to forgive so mean a crime. In the end "the old alliance in the face of Duncan's oppression rose between them"—and Sibyl won back her place in the family affection. We may remember that the Kent family lived on together for some years at Road, knowing that one of them had committed infanticide; and that Constance, who for religious reasons was later wrought up to confess her crime, was never able to prove it satisfactorily. Truth is stranger even than Miss Compton-Burnett's fiction.

The crimes in the remaining books are less co-ordinated. It was not Sir Jesse's tyranny that urged Ridley Cranmer, who was outside the family, to plan a bigamous marriage—but it gave him the opportunity. Eleanor Sullivan would have done much to leave the family home, and Ridley calculated that she would have remained with him even when her husband returned. But the Enoch Arden husband returns before the bigamous marriage takes place. This crime is a little hard to accept: the criminal had a good chance of getting away with it but it is hard to imagine Eleanor as exercising so powerful a temptation.

In *Elders and Betters*, Sukey Donne's practice of will-shaking enables her niece Anna to suppress her real will and to obtain the inheritance due to her other aunt, Jessica Calderon. Jessica suspects something of the truth and tries to wring a confession from Anna—who, in self-defence, so works upon the nerves of the over-scrupulous Jessica that she commits suicide. Anna is left undisturbed and unsuspected in the enjoyment of her ill-gotten gains: she can now afford to buy her cousin Terence, Jessica's charming young son, for a husband —and she does so. The book ends with the wicked flourishing like a green bay-tree.

The *New Statesman* reviewer "violently hoped for a quite different, a more vindictive ending": perhaps he wanted poetic justice. Other readers, though caring nothing for justice, may yet have looked forward to a superb *anagnorisis*. Miss Compton-Burnett had the strength of mind to refuse any concession and to deny herself the wonderful scene of discovery that she could so brilliantly have contrived:

"The *New Statesman* wanted wickedness to be punished, but my point is that it is not punished, and that is why it is natural to be guilty of it. When it is likely to be punished, most of us avoid it."

The next two books lack violent happenings and, for all their great beauty, their great perfection of texture, their aphoristic brilliance and their wonderful revelations of human nature, there is a lacuna. They do not quite rank with the great novels of this author: *Men and Wives*, *More Women Than Men*, *A House and Its Head*, *Daughters and Sons*, *A Family and a Fortune* and *Manservant and Maidservant*. Perhaps the author will make another return, as she did in *Manservant and Maidservant*, to her greatest theme.

*Two Worlds and Their Ways* is the story of two home-bred children, pushed by their parents' love and pride into a long course of cheating at their schools. The conflict between home and school is mercifully and quietly resolved. The coda, in which the butler is revealed to be their father's natural son and their mother is found to have stolen an ear-ring, unnecessarily weights the scales in the children's favour. It is ingeniously devised but it lacks necessity—like the coda about Sabine's will at the end of *Daughters and Sons*.

*Darkness and Day* takes rather a long time to get started. Edmund Lovat is shocked to find that his wife Bridget may be his natural daughter. His brother Gaunt makes a Sophoclean speech about it:

" 'If Edmund's daughters marry, their children will not only
be his grandchildren. And Bridget will not only be their
grandmother. Bridget has done and suffered the traditional
tragic things. As nearly the same as Oedipus as a woman could.
He killed his father and married his mother. And she caused
her mother's death when she was born, and married her
father. The difference is, as she said herself, that she has not
put out her eyes.' "

But after the darkness of uncertainty, daylight returns—
light is thrown on old, forgotten, far-off fornications and it is
seen that Bridget is not Edmund's daughter.

*The Present and the Past* is a more satisfying novel, with a
particularly well integrated plot. Cassius Clare has separated
by mutual consent from his first wife, Catherine, the mother of
his two elder boys; they have divorced and he has married
Flavia, by whom he has a second family. After nine years'
absence Catherine returns to the same village and begs to be
allowed to see her sons. After some preliminary jealousy, a
great friendship grows up between Catherine and Flavia;
Cassius, feeling neglected, stages an attempt at suicide to
restore his importance, but his fraud is detected. It recoils upon
him later, for when he sinks into a genuine coma he fails to
receive the immediate attention which would have saved him,
because the household think he is playing the same trick again.
After his death the two women break apart, feeling that the
tie between them exists no longer. Catherine asks to take her
two sons with her; Flavia gives them their choice. The elder,
Fabian, chooses his real mother; Guy, the younger, goes with a

broken heart from the stepmother who has brought him up because he cannot leave his brother: "I must go with Fabian. To live without him would be the same as being dead." The tragedy of the book lies in the helplessness of childhood, victimized by adult meetings and partings, but the author has some pity for poor, ineffective Cassius, a greater pity than she would probably have shown in her earlier books.

It is important to view the happenings in Miss Compton-Burnett's books rightly. The Crime Club attitude would be absurd: we are not to ask what drug Harriet took, what occurred at the inquests on her and on little Richard Edgeworth, or how the dangerous village talk died down without leading to a criminal investigation. These, and suchlike difficulties, are irrelevant to the main theme; we can believe that the author could—she is ingenious enough—have got round them if it had been her business to do so. What it is her business to do is to show that her happenings have issued naturally out of her people—and this she has, in almost every case, done. She need not tidy up after them.

On the other hand it is a mistake to dismiss the melodramatic framework as unimportant—as an inartistic device for stringing together wonderful and revealing scenes of human wickedness. Dickens cared little about his plots and Scott nothing for most of his love stories—but Miss Compton-Burnett is a neater and more conscientious artist. Her murders are probably as dear to her as were marriages to Jane Austen. She evidently believes that in them "there are signs that strange things happen".

There are signs indeed. Criminology generally takes us among the lower classes, and the majority of executed criminals seem to have been monsters: there are exceptions, and a few famous trials are worth reading from this point of view. "Nice people" are sometimes condemned, sometimes have a very narrow and perhaps an unmerited escape—this suggests that educated people are cleverer at crime, when they turn their minds to it. The cleverest of all are not even put on trial.

*Les Faux-Monnayeurs* has been regarded as a tissue of improbabilities: yet we know that it has been built up from facts and owes only too little to imagination. André Gide had a very strange suicide at Clermont-Ferrand as a precedent for his *crime immotive* and it received some *ex post facto* justification from the crime of Leopold and Loeb. But the crimes of Matthew Haslam, Josephine Napier and Sibyl Edgeworth are only too well motivated; they can also be justified by documentation if it is required.

Incest, common among the poor as a result of overcrowding, is probably rare among the "comfortable classes", though not unknown. Unwitting incest must always be possible when there are unowned natural children about. These phenomena are rarer in an age of divorce and of birth control but, as their name implies, it is natural for them to happen and we know they do.

We may think it strange that Sophia Stace never wondered if Christian were her father's son, and strange that Edmund Lovat did not find out more about Bridget's parentage—but it could have happened. We have only to read Mr Gerald Bullett's novel on the Theban theme, to find those of Miss Compton-Burnett prosaically probable by comparison.

"The *New Statesman* wanted wickedness to be punished, but my point is that it is not punished": documentation is not really to the point. We may get some confirmatory evidence if we read such trials as those of the Tichborne claimant, of

Madeleine Smith, of Dr Cross, of Constance Kent—or, in our own century, of Greenwood, of Armstrong, of Mrs Thompson and Bywaters, of Mrs Rattenbury and Stonor, and of Sidney Harry Fox. The cases that would be parallel are cases that have never come to trial.

More valuable information is given by memoirs and biographies, which may not record such happenings but show fields where they might so easily have occurred. Tennyson's drunken clerical father often threatened to put an end to his own existence and was locally (though unjustly) thought to have set fire to the cook; Branwell Brontë often retired for the night saying that this night would be the end of either his father or himself; who can doubt that wicked old Mr Barrett could have murdered Elizabeth, rather than let her escape, or that vile old Mrs Ruskin could have murdered Effie if she had not had other plans for the young wife's downfall? And as for the original of Christian Pontifex, she deserved to be murdered.

Most valuable is the confirmation given by hearsay, guesswork and experience. There are signs that strange things happen. From tombstones, parish registers, local talk and guesswork Hardy constructed the family-stories in *A Group of Noble Dames*: they are not pretty stories. If we remember everything we hear and if we use the sources of information that are open to everyone, such as reference books and old newspapers, it is quite astonishing what we can discover. We can even ask questions. "Ask no questions, hear no lies" —but "if you ask no questions, you have no truth told you either. It is surprising how much truth people tell: I would not if I were they. And you can get a lot of truth from the falsehoods they tell when you ask them questions. I admire them so much for telling them so awkwardly: I have a great respect for people."

Suicide, at any rate, is not uncommon—and when it happens we do not always find out as much as we should like about the motives. And there is more than one reason why a member of a family is never spoken of. The more we find out, the worse it generally seems to be. "*Non est curiosus, quin idem sit malevolus*", quotes Bacon: satisfied curiosity may give some people motives for envy but to more of us it gives motives for acute pity— we may come upon "a wonderful and startling thing and fraught with bitterness for others. It may make one's own lot better by comparison."

But no confirmation can take us to the bitter end; some of the very worst things are hushed up—"through long lives and on death-beds" they remain in darkness; one or two people keep the impossible secret until the grave covers it. The darkest of all places are often not even suspected; it is into these, the deepest oubliettes and dungeons of the Family, that Miss Compton-Burnett flashes her lantern. "Who has measured their depth?" She has. It is her distinction that she is one of the ultimate writers, one of those who tell us the very last things the human spirit is capable of in certain directions. Some even greater writers are not ultimate in this sense; Jane Austen is not, and perhaps few novelists have been—Conrad, perhaps, was such a novelist, Proust certainly was, and there is little doubt about Miss Compton-Burnett.

# CHAPTER 4

## *The Victims*

---

**(1)** *Adults and Adolescents*

MISS COMPTON-BURNETT IS not a novelist of the passions; but she is a novelist of the affections. Tyranny in the family is apt to unite the tyrant's victims by very strong ties. Elizabeth Barrett, herself a victim, wrote movingly to Robert Browning: "I told you once that we held hands the faster in this house for the weight over our heads." The love that exists between Miss Compton-Burnett's victims, particularly among the better characters among them, is as good as such a feeling can be, in fact or fiction.

In its strongest form, it is between two people of the same generation: Andrew and Dinah Stace, Jermyn and Griselda Haslam, Grant and Nance Edgeworth, Luce and Graham Sullivan—but it is not exclusive, it runs through the family and sometimes takes in a member of the older generation; a mother, like Ellen Edgeworth; a governess, like Cassandra Jekyll; an uncle, like Dudley Gaveston, and a cousin, like Mortimer Lamb.

The presence of this love lightens the tragedy of these books, makes them larger and more humane than *The Way of All Flesh*, that other exposure of family life with which it is natural to compare them. It provides the element of "desirable life" which Sainte-Beuve required in a novel and could not find in *Madame Bovary*. Moreover the tyrants themselves benefit by this affection, which is there ready to save them from themselves or to pick them up after a fall. This affection broods like a dove over the stormy waters of family life—it is the spirit, which, at the end, after the tempest, will produce calm and reconciliation.

Jane Austen set the same high value upon the affections and probably in her heart rated them above love itself—most of her heroines are hardly separated from their families by marriage. Elinor and Marianne live together in the same village of Delaford, one married to the squire and the other to the parson. Jane and Elizabeth Bennet settle within thirty miles of each other. Emma brings her husband to share her home with her old father. Fanny Price marries the cousin with whom she has been brought up from childhood and soon they are installed in the parsonage at Mansfield. But the conventions of her time and the exigencies of her plots made marriage the goal of Jane Austen's characters—for this cause they were ready to leave not only father and mother but also the dearest of sisters if need be. Miss Compton-Burnett, on the other hand, sees value in marriage chiefly because of the fraternal relation it will give rise to in the next generation—and which it often seems to produce between husband and wife as the years pass. It is no doubt deliberate irony that her married couple who are the most truly husband and wife are Christian and Sophia Stace, they who are also brother and sister.

The incests in her books are partly explained by the fact that the family tie can be so strong. Christian and Sophia almost inevitably become husband and wife because they do not know that they are brother and sister; the converse process happens, and when the Langs find that they cannot marry the Staces they become their brother and sister.

Grant Edgeworth is more or less ordered by Duncan to marry one of his daughters, one of the cousins with whom he has been brought up: he is quite willing to do so, and first offers himself to Nance. The proposal is not passionate but it would be hard to find one in literature in which affection is stronger and more sincere:

" 'You can't say you do not love me. We could not have lived in this house for all these years, without mutual affection; Uncle would have made it impossible: I think he has a right to expect us to marry.' "

Ernest Pontifex, in *The Way of All Flesh*, was always suffering from fraternal treachery and meanness. This is a thing almost unknown in Miss Compton-Burnett's Unhappy Families. True, Anna Donne is sometimes a hectoring elder sister, and Clement Gaveston and Esmond Donne are rough with their charming younger brothers, Aubrey and Reuben. Chilton Ponsonby has a facetious habit of badgering his younger brother Victor, and much the same relation exists between Daniel and Graham Sullivan—but Daniel and Graham are fond of each other and Victor is a very stolid boy; in neither case is there any harm done.

Anyone who is a favourite with a parent seems to use that position well: it is always regarded as a position of responsibility rather than of privilege. Andrew Stace exercises some tender restraint upon Sophia and Gregory Haslam's devotion to Harriet spares his family a great deal of strain. France Ponsonby has much to put up with as a result of being her father's favourite: her aunt is jealous of their affection and her father is jealous of her literary talent. Some daughters, however, like to fancy themselves greater favourites with their fathers than they really are—such are Sibyl Edgeworth, Justine Gaveston and even Tullia Calderon (though she really is a favourite).

Among the victims there is a very high level of human goodness, more than enough to raise their average, even though there are two murderers among them. Their care for their younger and even more helpless brothers and sisters is to be noted. Even constipated, apathetic Clare Ponsonby is roused to action when Muriel is being bullied by grown-up unimaginativeness.

" 'Leave her alone, Aunt Hetta,' said Clare. 'What good does it do to torment her?'

" 'Are you the mistress of the house?'

" 'Yes, I am, when you and Grandma fail in the part. I come next. Muriel, you can go to bed, and you need not say good night.' "

In the great symphony of young voices in *Parents and Children* it is easy to lose any single voice, but on subsequent readings, if each time a different voice is followed, there are new revelations to be gained. It is worth listening particularly to the "deep, jerky voice" of Graham Sullivan; he is his grandfather's victim and his elder brother's butt—his sister Luce has an especial gentleness with him and compassion on his tender-heartedness. If it can ever be said of anyone that he is tender-hearted to a fault, then it can be said of Graham—his heart is wrung by the very comfortable and complacent governess who would be exceedingly sorry to have to change places with him—his heart is wrung even by the exposure of Ridley's bigamous designs on his mother. When the news of his father's death comes, he is quick to volunteer to break it to the younger children to spare them the scene that their mother will make of it. He is particularly careful to come between trouble and his young brother James, another unfortunate member of the family.

Another such a gentle and tender-hearted young man is Terence Calderon in *Elders and Betters*: his position is a good deal better than that of Graham Sullivan, for he is the elder son and his mother's favourite, and has a sharp wit with which to defend himself. The family governess is obviously thick-skinned and so (in their odd way) are his youngers and inferiors—except in things due to the helplessness of childhood. On this he takes compassion, and deserves and wins their love. He also wins the reader's love, and it is a bitter moment when the author allows his abominable cousin Anna to buy Terence for a husband.

Aubrey Gaveston, in *A Family and A Fortune*, is a touchingly tender-hearted boy of fifteen: his pity must all be for his elders, as he is the youngest character in the book, and often they require his pity. He fights this feeling sometimes, when it becomes overpowering, with bright, facetious little remarks in a shaking voice:

" 'My dear,' [says someone unnamed, but almost certainly his sister Justine], 'think what you are saying. What makes you talk like that?'

" 'Excess of feeling and a wish to disguise it,' said Aubrey, but not aloud."

There is a lovely passage with his stepmother:

" 'Quickly up and quickly down at my age. But if I am thought callous one minute, I am thought sensitive the next.'

" 'We need not mind being thought callous sometimes,' said Maria, seeing the aspect preferred.

" 'No. The heart knoweth,' said her stepson, turning away."

Many of Miss Compton-Burnett's characters wring our hearts, but perhaps there are only two who often draw tears —these are Aubrey and his uncle Dudley, whom he both resembles and imitates.

Dudley is not strictly a victim; he belongs to an older generation and is one of the few people to whom the terrible Matty behaves well. But a victim he is, of circumstances and of his own good nature, doomed always to come second to his elder brother Edgar who is in most ways inferior to him— though it is too much to say (with Miss Hansford-Johnson) that he is not "worth his little finger"; Edgar is a worthy, upright man.

The beauty of Dudley's love for Edgar, and even of the return that Edgar makes to it, shows that the young have not the monopoly of fraternal love—though Hetta's love for her brother has become tyrannical and oppressive, and the sisterly relation between Matty Seaton and Blanche Gaveston has not much to commend it.

## (2) *Children*

Schoolroom and nursery children are often remoter victims than the grown-up or half grown-up young: they are spared a great deal when they do not eat in the dining-room—so many terrible things happen when the whole family is assembled for meals.

Muriel Ponsonby is eleven, but she is in the dining-room for breakfast, the danger hour, and for luncheon: on family occasions, always dangerous occasions, she comes down to dinner as well.

Muriel is complacent, if inarticulate, and suffers less than most children would, though much exposed to that form of cruelty to children described by Wordsworth in *Anecdote for Fathers*. This is a bad poem, but that is not the only reason why it is distressing.

> " 'Now, little Edward, say why so:
> My little Edward, tell me why.'—
> 'I cannot tell, I do not know.'—
> 'Why, this is strange,' said I. . . .
> At this, my boy hung down his head,
> He blushed with shame, nor made reply;
> And three times to the child I said,
> 'Why, Edward, tell me why?' "

The child, forced to say something, made a silly answer: Wordsworth, unlike the Ponsonby family, learned his lesson. He headed his poem with this pathetic epigraph: *"Retine vim istam, falsa enim dicam si coges."*

Muriel, however, is in her way a martyr to truth: she will not speak the speeches they want to put into her mouth.

" 'Muriel, you may say to Father that you are so pleased about his present, and you think he more than deserves it.'

" 'I don't want to, Aunt Hetta.'

" 'Why not?'
" 'Because I don't say things like that.' "

This is one of the many passages in Miss Compton-Burnett's books that anyone who is about to become a parent, a grand-parent, a step-parent, an uncle or aunt, a tutor or governess, ought to read and take humbly to heart. And no diploma in education ought to be given except after a course in which she is a compulsory set author.

"A Man shall see", said Bacon in his essay *Of Parents and Children*, "where there is a house full of *Children*, one or two, of the Eldest, respected, and the Youngest made wantons; But in the middest, some that are, as it were forgotten, who, many times, neverthelesse, prove the best." In Miss Compton-Burnett's novel, *Parents and Children*, a wide range of family relationships is explored: there are nine young Sullivans, three in the dining-room, three in the school-room, and three in the nursery. Daniel and Luce, the eldest two, are respected; we have already seen Graham's position; Nevill, the youngest, is self-protected by a wilfully and carefully prolonged babyhood—it is understandable that he is in no hurry to share the life of the remaining five.

From these come utterances of a terrible childish wisdom, a new thing in her work, though children had been introduced before.

Gavin (aged nine) says to Eleanor, his well-meaning but imperceptive mother: "It is the person you are talking to, that you don't think is easy." Honor, a year older, comments on the going out of mourning for their father: "We went out because Mother was going to marry again. The children can't

58

look as if they still minded, when the mother has proved that she doesn't." Isabel, aged fifteen, when asked by her mother to tell her thoughts, replies: "You should not want to know the things in people's minds. If you were meant to hear them, they would be said." The most terrible and wise saying of all is that of Gavin: he says he would like to die when he cannot get anyone to believe his story, his story of the evidence of his own senses, "because as long as you are alive, things can happen that you don't like. Even if you couldn't bear them, they would happen."

In *Elders and Betters*, Reuben Donne is lame and pathetic—but his cousins, Julius and Theodora Calderon, react vigorously against the plight of childhood. They resist, like a very tough, conquered race, but, like all children, are a conquered race at best.

"Their pastimes included not only pleasure, but religion, literature and crime. They wrote moral poems that deeply moved them, pilfered coins for the purchase of forbidden goods, and prayed in good faith to the accepted god and their own, perhaps with a feeling that a double share of absolution would not come amiss."

The scenes in which they pray to their private god are among the most wonderful revelations of the child-mind in literature —the exact degree of earnestness, play-acting, and suspension of disbelief are all there. This is the prayer of Julius and Dora, after their aunt has died suddenly, and their mother has poisoned herself.

" 'O great and good and powerful god, Chung, grant that our life may not remain clouded, as it is at this present. And

grant that someone may guide us in the manner of our mother,
so that we may not wander without direction in the maze of
life. For although we would have freedom, if it be thy will,
yet would we be worthy of being our mother's children. And
if there is danger of our inheriting the weaknesses of our
mother and aunt, thy late handmaids, guard us from them, O
god, and grant that we may live to a ripe old age. For it
would not be worth while to suffer the trials of childhood, if
they were not to lead to fullness of days. And we pray to thee
to comfort our father and our brother and sister; and if they
are less in need of comfort than beseems them, pardon them,
O god, and lead them to know the elevation of true grief.'

"Dora's voice trembled for the first time, and her brother
took his hands from his face and gave her a look of approval.

" 'And grant that our father may not form the habit of
talking of our mother, and thus cast a cloud upon us; but
rather may lock up all such things in his heart, and commune
solely with himself upon them, so that his heart may know its
own bitterness. Nevertheless not as we will, but as thou wilt.
For Si Lung's sake, amen.'

" 'We are more likely to have our prayers granted, for not
insisting upon it,' said Julius.

" 'And weaknesses is a good word for the causes of Aunt
Sukey's dying and Mother's. It takes in everything, and does
not call attention to things we should not know. It would not
do to obtrude our knowledge, as if we were proud of it.'

" 'It is really better if Mother did not die of natural causes,'
said Julius, 'because those are the ones you can inherit.'

" 'It is strange how, as we get older, our requests take on a
touch of maturity,' said Dora, investing her tone with the same
touch.

" 'It is passing strange,' said Julius. 'Verily we are having a unique childhood.' "

This is a breath-taking scene; it could only be the work of great creative genius. Unperceptive readers probably dismiss Julius and Dora as little monsters—but they have their pathos as well as their humour. "It would not be worth while to suffer the trials of childhood, if they were not to lead to fullness of days"—that is the very voice of Childhood speaking. And the private religion is not only a relief to them, it is their chief means of communication with each other; things they could not say to each other they can say to Chung.

The most dreadfully driven children are those in *Manservant and Maidservant*: they shiver in an unwarmed schoolroom, come out of church before the sermon to hide their shabby clothes,[1] are badgered and bullied by Horace Lamb and are then asked to show gratitude for it. No wonder their mother, who owns the money, thinks of eloping with Mortimer, who would be kind to them: no wonder Marcus and Jasper think of their father's death as a deliverance—unfortunately this thought is revealed.

" 'It was only for a minute that we waited,' said Marcus; 'and then we wished we had spoken. It did seem that, if you did not come back, the other times could not come back either. It had seemed that they might be coming. And we felt we could not bear it.'

" 'So you would have no father, rather than the one you once

---

[1] Miss Hansford-Johnson says that Marcus and Jasper "have obviously been over-exposed every Sunday morning to sermons intended for adults".

had,' said Horace sadly, looking into their faces. 'But was that a fair way to deal with him? Just to do him to death? Could you not give him a chance? Could you not say a word of help? What would happen to you, if I took the line with you, that you take with me?'

" 'We are afraid of you. You know we are,' said Marcus. 'Your being different for a little while has not altered all that went before. Nothing can alter it. You did not let us have anything; you would not let us be ourselves. If it had not been for Mother, we would rather have been dead. It was feeling like that so often, that made us think dying an ordinary thing. We had often wished to die ourselves. It is not the same with you as with other people. If anyone else did something, we should just see that thing. If you do it, it adds itself to all the rest. We cannot help it. Neither can you help it now. It is something that cannot be changed.' "

Marcus, this brave and upright spokesman for his brother and himself, may grow up with Dudley's quiet heroism: his father thinks him a juvenile delinquent.

Sefton and Clemence Shelley, in *Two Worlds and Their Ways*, have a very kind home but they get into trouble at their schools: they have much terrible, childish wisdom to utter.

" 'Shall we ever be happy again, quite happy as we used to be?'

" 'It will take some time. But we shall get nearer to it. Though perhaps we were hardly as happy as we think now.

It will be difficult to judge, now that we have known something else.' "

" 'I know such a lot of unexpected things. Things that are said and not thought, and things that are thought and not said. And there are so many of both.' "

Henry, in *The Present and the Past*, who begins the book with his habitual cry of: "Oh, dear, oh dear!" is a natural pessimist, and terrible in his wisdom. He can, at the age of eight, say of his little brother: "Toby doesn't know that things as they are, are all that is. He can still believe anything and be happy."

### (3) *Governesses*

After children have suffered so much, they can be forgiven if they inflict some suffering in their turn: the governesses are these little tyrants' victims. A governess, however, can leave, as a child cannot: moreover it is only those who fail in knowledge or character who have to suffer because they are not fit for their places. Edith Hallam, Miss Mitford, Miss Lacy and Miss Ridley are successful and respected.

Miss Bunyan in *Daughters and Sons* is the exception, in that she is the grandmother's victim rather than her pupil's. She is silly, snobbish, and a heavy eater: Sabine Ponsonby snubs her social aspirations and caters for her appetite while drawing attention to it. Muriel giggles at her every mouthful.

" 'Governesses are always concerned about what they eat,' said Sabine . . . 'they find themselves where the food is better than in their homes, and they have no other interest in their lives.' "

" 'I have had two governesses,' said Honor Sullivan. 'I know the tricks of the trade. . . . And the nature of the beasts.' "

We see her trying to break in Miss Pilbeam, whose "qualification for teaching was her being supposed to know more than young children": Honor is ten and her brother Gavin nine, and Honor at least is intelligent enough to think little of her governess's qualification. But Miss Pilbeam is an unpretending young woman and manages to defend her ground.

Mildred Hallam, in *Darkness and Day*, has her task made harder by her own cocksureness and by even more difficult children who intend to get rid of her and to return to lessons with Fanshawe, their nurse.

" 'You think you are patient,' said Viola, wiping her brush. 'But I can tell from your voice that you are not.'

" 'Well, people's patience does not last forever. It is as well to learn that.'

" 'Yours did not last even for half-an-hour,' said Rose, looking at the clock. 'We have never had anyone with so little.'

" 'I have any amount, if there is a reasonable demand on it.'

" 'Well, then you would not need it.'

" 'And you have even less than you pretend to have,' said Viola.

" 'And so I suppose you expect me to lose it?'

" 'Well, we were waiting for that,' said Viola, in an almost engaging tone.

" 'And then what is to happen?' said Mildred.

" 'You will say you can't teach us, and stop coming, and

we shall go back to learning with Fanshawe. But I daresay you will have your pay for the month. The last governess did.' "

In the awkward position of the governess, between family and servants, treated as a member of the family, and even worse than the family, are two other victims. There is Miss Griffin, companion and slave to the terrible Aunt Matty—badgered and stormed at and finally driven out into the snow. There is Miss Patmore, "mother's help" to Sophia Stace, who serves her devotedly for more than twenty-eight years and suddenly regains a life of her own at Sophia's death—she is then almost indecently elated.

Although some of these victims may be roughly classifiable in "character-types", yet there is great diversity within the types. Miss Hansford-Johnson exhibits four governesses at work: Mildred Hallam, Miss Pilbeam, Edith Hallam, Miss Lacy. She observes: "So far as the teaching methods are concerned, the psychological approach, the method of gaining authority, the cadence of speech, each of these four governesses could be transferred out of one book into the other without anybody being the wiser."

In fact, a perceptive reader of the four passages that she excerpts, none of them much more than fifty words long, could unerringly pick out the two women he would be willing to employ and the two that he would not. Very likely he could put the four women in order of merit: that is not easy for a reader to determine who does not come fresh to these extracts and already knows each governess as a distinctive character.

### (4) *Servants*

There is a strict hierarchy below-stairs. Generally the lives of cook and butler are easy enough and are perhaps the most enviable lives in the novels. Such butlers as Jellamy, Buttermere and Bullivant are even intimidating to their masters—so is such a very superior parlour-maid as the Edgeworths' Bethia or the Chaces' Jennet. Even if not intimidated, tyrants upstairs are often considerate to servants, who could give notice; they often pride themselves unduly on this considerateness.

The really victimized servants are those who are tyrannized over by their fellow-servants. Life below-stairs is a commentary on life above-stairs—the despotism of the cook and butler in the servants' hall is a kind of parody of the tyranny that goes on in the dining-room. It is a comic under-plot to the tragic plot enacting upstairs—as in Elizabethan drama the low life parodies the high life. It is comic, because so much milder—if the young footman thinks the butler a beast, he probably thinks him a just beast; and the cook, like most good cooks (and she is probably a good cook, for the Unhappy Families always appear to have rather good food), has a motherly heart.

George, in *Manservant and Maidservant*, is not a very nice young footman: his life is pitiful, but he forfeits pity by trying to take out upon others his own humiliations—he snubs the girl, Miriam, who is his junior and he is ready to lay the blame for his delinquencies upon the children of the house, who are even more pitiful and powerless than he. His attempt upon his master's life, which is full of self-dramatization, has an unreality which makes it more easily forgivable than his real meanness to Jasper and Marcus.

Bartle, on the other hand, in *Darkness and Day*, is touching

66

in his attempts to assert himself and to talk more grandly: even his insatiable curiosity is sympathetic—there are certainly things to know in the Lovat household—and it is gratifying that the upper servants never manage to thwart it and never can keep down his spirit.

Of servants, Miss Compton-Burnett said in the *Conversation*: "I feel I have a knowledge of servants in so far as they take a part in the world they serve. This may mean that the knowledge is superficial, as I have thought it in other people's books."

This was before her servants'-hall scenes, in which she shows a knowledge very far from superficial. In Jane Austen's novels servants are kept behind the scenes—though Mrs Bennet's housekeeper, Mrs Hill, takes an interest in Lydia's elopement, and Thomas, Mrs Dashwood's manservant, so far forgets himself, while waiting at table, as to announce Lucy Steele's marriage. Their characters are not indicated, for it was not necessary to Jane Austen's purpose: nor do we know anything about Mr Knightley's William Larkins nor Miss Bates's Patty. Miss Compton-Burnett has a Proustian knowledge of the servants' hall—and, like Proust, has here learned something from Dickens. And surely every novelist, in his heart, must want people to find in him affinities to Dickens? One could take very little interest in a novelist who altogether lacked that ambition.

# CHAPTER 5

## *The Chorus*

THE TRAGEDY OF tyrant and victim is encompassed by witnesses: they are on the whole powerless to help or hinder, as a Greek chorus is—though this is not an unbreakable rule. Pity or sympathy they can give, and some of them give it to the wrong side—and they have the passionate curiosity of a Greek chorus, as well they may, when they are so often on the track of similar secrets. They mass, like a chorus, to form an audience for family scenes: but they do not speak like a chorus—each witness has his own clear voice. They consist, as in Greek tragedy, of the people living in the place where the action occurs; we can even include among them the more aloof members of the stricken household who have no very close connection with its drama. *Two Worlds and Their Ways* seems to have both a home chorus and a semi-chorus provided by each school.

Though the witnesses may be roughly grouped for purposes of convenience in a few categories, it must be emphasized, firstly, that this grouping is not exclusive or all-embracing; next, that it classifies the witnesses according to their functions in the main story and not according to character-types; for the witnesses, like the tyrants and their victims, are far more individual than critics will readily allow: it is their conduct rather than their character that permits us to distinguish some of them as the Curious, the Prigs, the Toadies, the Good Governesses, the Aloof, and the Lower Classes. Characters in the first five of these categories are, of course, there because of some trait of *character* in the first place; but within each of these categories there is a great variety of character. Few, if any, of this author's characters are merely *characters* (in the sense of "humours").

## (1) *The Curious*

On the whole, these are good characters: they are frank enough not to dissemble the curiosity which it would be inhuman not to feel if one lived in proximity to any of Miss Compton-Burnett's Unhappy Families. Few writers have so relaxed the tabu against curiosity. Where it is not condemned as mean it is generally despised as vulgar; but Miss Compton-Burnett recognizes it as a great human need, if rather a comical one.

Rachel Hardisty, in *Men and Wives*, is lucky enough to be able to satisfy that need; she says of the less lucky members of her family: "I hate to think of their not knowing the best part (about Harriet's attempted suicide); but denying ourselves the relation of it will be atonement. . . . But people will not realize that the pleasure of being well-informed should be intellectual; they make it social."

It is a social pleasure too: Julian Wake has a tea-party directly it comes out that Mrs Lang is Christian Stace's mother and that the young Langs can therefore not marry the young Staces—"we can't put gossip off until we return from London. It has a frail hold on life like all precious things."

Among other people, they ask the priggish Drydens. ". . . [Judith] and Edward will sit and not say a word about the subject, and feel that keeping off it is elevating. And sitting, doing that, seems worse than just doing it. It seems to imply a breach of the rules of hospitality. And I find keeping off it lowering."

We see the prigs and the honestly curious getting down to the subject.

" 'Why should we talk about it?' said Edward, revealing that he knew what the matter was.

" 'It is not a particularly interesting thing to talk about,' said Judith."

[A typically English piece of hypocrisy, likely to come out when any really absorbing personal topic is under discussion. Compare: "We never speak of it"—which means: "We hardly ever speak of anything else."]

" 'I think that is just what it is,' said Sarah.

" 'Do you, Sarah?' said Edward. 'I should have thought you would feel it better not to discuss the affairs of our friends, when they are painful for them, and nothing to do with us . . .'

" 'Oh, but gossiping about people, and gloating over their difficulties, and indulging in a sort of offensive pity is such an average sort of thing,' said Judith.

" 'I don't think it is at all. Most people are a long way above that,' said Sarah."

"Simple, candid probing of our friends' business" is how

Julian describes his tea-party to Caroline Lang. But there is no kinder friend and neighbour than Julian: the Drydens, on the other hand, run away from scandal rather than stick to their friends who are facing it.

A chorus of the curious gather outside the Ponsonbys' gate, drawn by the news of John's marriage: Miss Marcon, Sir Rowland Seymour and his son Evelyn are the friendly vultures (and very good friends they all prove themselves). They parley a little, before going in.

". . . 'We can't arrive in a body to ask questions.'

" 'No, no, not in a body, no. But we want to ask some questions; yes, I think we do.'

" 'To find out about the marriage we have seen in the papers. How else are we to know about it? It is a wonderful and startling thing and fraught with bitterness for others. It may make one's own lot better by comparison.'

" 'Now what exactly do you want to know? If you wait here, I will come and tell you. Things are not so good at second hand, but they are better than nothing, so much better.'

" 'We want to know the whole thing,' said Evelyn. 'Our curiosity is neither morbid nor ordinary. It is the kind known as devouring. We want you to be completely satisfying. It is awful not to be satisfied.' "

These are the subtler curious, something feline mingles with their curiosity, which is not, of course, the whole of their character. It is, on the other hand, nearly the whole of the character of Sarah Middleton, in *A Family and A Fortune*, who is mainly animated by a pure desire for knowledge about other people's affairs.

" 'I don't like things to pass me by, without my hearing about them. We are meant to be interested in what the Almighty ordains.' "

### (2) *The Toadies*

The form of doubleness and moral cowardice characteristic of a toady is admirably illustrated in *Pastors and Masters* in the person of Mr Merry, the first of the species to appear in these novels: he combines the function of toady with the office of schoolmaster in a private school. He is a toady in the soul, so that he does not only abase himself before power (his employer's family and the boys' parents) but also before his wife, the junior staff and the servants—almost before the boys.

"Mr Merry, a tall, thin man about fifty, leaned back in his chair, and fixed on his pupils his little, pale, screwed up eyes, to which he had the gift of imparting an alluring kindness." (He bears some resemblance to Mr Bode, in *A House and Its Head*: "a tall, stooping man about fifty, with a small mottled face and an affectionate manner." Mr Bode had lately retired from a profession: one would guess that it had been schoolmastering—one would also guess that the same model had been behind the original conception of each of these characters, though they have been differently worked up.)

Every speech of Mr Merry reveals his weakness.

" 'Mother, ought not Mr Burgess' bacon to be kept hot?'

said Mr Merry, his voice conveying criticism of Mr Burgess, and the need of diplomacy with him.

" 'We do not usually expect people to come down when breakfast is over,' said Mrs Merry. 'The bacon was hot when it was brought in.'

" 'Fanny,' said Mr Merry, in a tone of apology to the maid who was waiting, 'just put Mr Burgess' bacon down in the fender, will you. Thank you, Fanny, very much.' "

The formula, "Thank you, Fanny, very much", several times repeated, is enough to stamp Mr Merry.

Dominic Spong, in *Men and Wives*, is in the fit place for a toady, "ranged on the side of power"; sometimes, like a toad, we see him swell. He patronizes anyone who is not in power—these happen to include Jane Austen herself ("I feel I must become acquainted with the fair writer"). He tends to equate the power that he serves with righteousness—and much in Lady Haslam is righteous. Of his own kind of smarminess, he is at once aware and tolerant. Though a prig also, he is humanly weak—and he ends by marrying Camilla, who has been "light", proving that he was right in hoping that he could hate the sin and love the sinner.

Spong is the family lawyer. Chaucer, in *Daughters and Sons*, the clergyman of the parish, has some resemblance to him: he repeats the names of people to whom he is speaking, fusses over minor gallantries, ranges himself firmly on the side of power, and, because that power is vested in women, thinks himself a chivalrous man. With his baby face, he is marked off from Spong, who wears a reproachful expression—and their speech fits their different faces and their different avocations. Chaucer comes off worse than Spong, for he marries Hetta Ponsonby.

Alfred Marcon, in the same book, is a pleasanter character: he sincerely admires old Mrs Ponsonby as a grand survival of an era that was in some ways finer than his own. He does not help her in any of her acts of tyranny; she needs no help—and though he does not help her victims they do not need it either, and his presence lightens the atmosphere for them. When at the end of the book he shows an unattractive acquisitiveness it is only because he has been unfairly caught out by circumstances.

## (3) *The Prigs*

This is a looser classification. There are prigs of many kinds. Edward Dryden, whose "self-esteem is so deep, that he has never even seen it", represents one sort of prig, and his sister Judith is the female variant—a little shriller but rather less objectionable. Sophia Stace thought them too shallow to be fit partners for her son and daughter and she was not wrong.

Women who do "good works" form another category: the poor, no doubt, must be clothed, but woe unto them that clothe them!

A men's class, her "dear men things", is Lydia Fletcher's form of good works. In *Men and Wives* Lady Haslam has a working-party, attended by some very terrible and very pathetic women. Agatha Calkin is a very prominent member. She also might be classified as a snob: she is an "experience" snob—anxious to claim intimacy with anyone whom some experience has made specially interesting. Mrs Spong, for instance, had just died: "Only last week I spent an hour with

74

her," says Agatha. "We had tea together on Thursday, just she and I. We had a very long talk. I am very glad I had it. I was very fond of her. Poor Lucy Spong!" Lady Haslam has gone into a mental home: "I was in her house the day after the dinner, and she told me a little about herself." We know how very little about herself Harriet Haslam would have told Agatha, and we discount, therefore, the intimacy with Lucy Spong—although we never knew her.

Another form of her "experience" snobbery is Agatha's extravagant claim to experience as a widow and mother. This is combined with priggishness of expression: she will refer to "the loss that no one knows who has not suffered it."

From this springs her feeling that she is almost more than a mother to Gregory Haslam and her boasts of his dependence on her. But she fails him when he wants her to help him to understand his mother's death—which he believes to be suicide.

" 'Would you dare to do it?' said Gregory.

" 'It is not a question of daring to do it,' said Agatha, lifting her head. 'It is a question rather of daring not to do it. Ah, I remember when my husband died. It did take some daring.'

" 'Are you speaking honestly?' said Gregory."

Gregory finally repudiates Agatha, very gently, but very publicly—just as she has in public staked a claim to his confidence.

" 'I daresay you were not thinking of what you were saying, but if you were, I have let you make a mistake. You will allow me to put it right, as the mistake is mine. No one can take the place of my mother to me. You would have seen that, if it had not been for me . . .' "

Agatha takes the rebuff heroically—and gently passes Gregory on to the girl of his own age, whose companionship is now what he needs.

Her younger sister, Geraldine Dabis, is more of an exhibitionist. "It is foolish," says Rachel Hardisty, "to dislike Agatha for having been married, and Geraldine for not having been. That is what they are disliked for. I don't dislike them for those reasons at all."

As an assertion of pride in her spinsterhood, Geraldine fancies she has a man's mind; she is even pleased when she has to make men's costumes for some amateur theatricals: "I always seem to get masculine habiliments for my portion! I don't know why they should be assigned especially to me."

As her elder sister makes so much of having been a wife and mother, Geraldine makes an assertion of greater sensitiveness, to compensate for less experience: "I have always been the most impossible burden at my times of stress, utterly unable to raise myself from the depths." "I can only remember writhing in darkness."

Writhe, Geraldine may well have done—everyone has had plenty to writhe about, whether or not a widow and mother. She is apt to gesticulate with her long hands and to raise her voice to hold her position in talk. But she subdues her gestures and her voice, observing Mrs Christy who is underbred and much more of a clown. Geraldine wishes to avoid resembling Mrs Christy, while her half-sister Kate imitates Rachel Hardisty: this trick of the author's, while giving the characters a superficial likeness, really further distinguishes them—it could not be played if we had not a firm idea of the separate personalities of Rachel and Kate, of Geraldine and Mrs Christy.

In this novel alone, the group of minor characters only (excluding the great figure of Harriet) probably contains more memorable people than could be mustered together out of the whole work of any other living novelist.

*A House and Its Head* has a remorseless trio of village philanthropists. There are the two "redoubtable cousins": Rosamund Burtenshaw, who, rather engagingly, "had retired from missionary work owing to the discomfort of the life, a reason which she did not disclose, though it was more than adequate; and was accustomed to say she found plenty of furrows to plough in the home field", and Beatrice Fellowes, who "at once served, admired and emulated her". Dulcia Bode, a girl of twenty-four, leagues herself with them.

Beatrice recalls Lydia Fletcher, almost seems to be a younger and more absurd version of the same character. Both are clumsy in appearance and have a similar, pious turn of speech.

Beatrice and Rosamund share a devotion to the clergyman of the parish, and when they lose him (by marriage to another woman) their reaction is given with great truth and humanity: they are "bound by mutual sympathy, mutual relief that neither was preferred to her friend, and a deep, almost subconscious gladness that their life was to remain unchanged."

Dulcia is a more independent character; there is no pathos about her—the violence of her reactions to the drama of other people's lives leaves her no emotion to spend on her own. She really has, about private life, the kind of feelings that the cheaper newspapers think it suitable to express about public events. That is, no doubt, one of the reasons why her speech abounds in clichés. Being quite unusually unsubtle and insensitive, she prides herself (as the stupid so often do) on her intuition about other people—she often expects their motives to be exaggeratedly noble—and labours under the delusion that this is the best friendship. She is one of the most interesting of the witnesses—and the author has never drawn another character the least bit like her.

The prig's function seems to have dropped out of the later novels—perhaps because they are full of children, compared with whose downrightness (Miss Hansford-Johnson prefers to call it "heartlessness") we are all of us more or less prigs. The last prig is perhaps Faith Cranmer in *Parents and Children* —she is a "Cruelty to Animals" prig and has the illusion that she is good with children, an illusion they do not share. "Not a high type", one of the young Sullivans sums her up.

## (4) *The Good Governesses*

These are (generally) governesses who, so far from being victims, are able by force of character to make a privileged position out of their status in the family. They are sufficiently of the family to know the worst and sufficiently detached from it to be willing and able to undo some of the effects of its wickedness.

Two of the noblest of these characters, Cassandra Jekyll and

Edith Hallam, marry the widowed fathers of their pupils. But even after marriage into the family they both retain a kind of visiting status, imposing no authority and remaining outside the original family—as Maria Sloane also does when she marries Edgar Gaveston. It is strange that in all the family relations she has explored Miss Compton-Burnett has not given us a wicked stepmother or a new sister-in-law who upsets everything by her entry into the family: her Unhappy Families are already set, and her sympathies are on the side of the newcomers who always have difficulty in entering the already crowded scene.

Miss Mitford in *Parents and Children* is more detached; there is not much that she can do for the victims, though some of them, rightly, prefer her to their mother.

At a family crisis: "Miss Mitford sat down to await the end of the scene. She did not leave it, because of its human appeal. She was the happiest person present, as she was more often than was suspected. She did not let pity for her employer or pupil mar her interest. Pity had come to be the normal background of her mind, and other feelings arose irrespective of it."

Here is the sort of disposition with which we should read these books—perhaps it is not unlike the disposition with which some of the later novels have been written.

Miss Lacy, in *Elders and Betters*, carries detachment (or the affectation of it) unnaturally far and sometimes causes the embarrassment which she is studying to avoid.

" 'Well, my niece and I have come to spend an hour with you. We are getting tired of each other's company, and are glad of friends at so easy a distance.' "

This is her greeting to the Calderon family, shocked and shaken by Jessica's suicide. One can sympathize with Terence Calderon's previous criticism of Miss Lacy: "Acting should only be carried to the proper point."

The other household in the same book is blessed with a housekeeper whose character is in this respect the opposite of Miss Lacy's. "Her position between the family and them (the servants) gave her an opportunity for living in two sets of lives, and she could not have lived in too many." Jenney is the general shock-absorber and in particular is the protector of the small lame boy, Reuben: insensitive characters, like Claribel and Anna, regard her as of a coarser mould than their own, as genuine Marthas are often regarded by those who labour under the delusion that they are Marys. The servants, who cannot help seeing profoundly into the running of the household, rightly regard her as a saint.

Another worthy but rather aloof governess is Miss Ridley, in *The Present and the Past*: "Her life was divided between her conscience and her inclination; it was her concern to strike the mean between them, and her merit that she did so."

A humbler member of this class is the nurse in *Manservant and Maidservant* who so nobly and movingly defends Marcus and Jasper.

First she defends them against themselves: "You would never have harmed your father, and you must not make a false memory. We cannot always control our thoughts, but they need not pass into action. We all mean to do things that we could not do, good things as well as bad. Have you not imagined yourselves heroes or martyrs or some other sort of great man? . . . And you know in your hearts that you will never be any such things? . . . That is how it was with this."

With equal vigour, she defends them against their father, and states her credentials: "Of course I do not watch them every minute of the day, they are past the age for that; but I know them as only a woman can, who lives with them hour by hour, and of whom they have no fear. Better than you do, sir, better than you ever can. I have a right to say what I know, and a right to expect a hearing."

At the two schools, in *Two Worlds and Their Ways*, it is the matrons who perform a similar function. When the two victims are having a sad conversation after their downfall, Clemence Shelley says: "You could hardly be a matron unless you were nice. You are always doing things for other people, that don't make you thought any more of, yourself."

Her brother answers, with terrible childish wisdom: "It seems that the nicest people don't have the important places. Perhaps the others know how to get them for themselves."

(5) *The Aloof*

Some of these are genuinely aloof from the struggle of life.

"The sight of duty does make one shiver," is appropriately the first utterance of Emily Herrick in *Pastors and Masters*. "The actual doing of it would kill one, I think."

She was "a tall, dark woman of fifty . . . with a face that somehow recalled an attractive idol's, iron-grey hair wound in plaits round her head, and a quick, deep voice".

Juliet Cassidy, in *Two Worlds and Their Ways*, is rather like Emily: she was "a plainer, feminine counterpart of her father and nephew", who were "large, dark men, with heavy, aquiline faces, dark, heavy-lidded eyes"—indeed, not unlike some idols. She had "an air of being clever, complacent and dissatisfied, and was all these things and would have denied none."

Aloof as they are, both of these women are swift in action when it is necessary to prevent a fraud from being embarrassingly exposed, for they are really kind—and their aloof, cynical cleverness is the quality most useful in the detection of fraud.

Miss Hansford-Johnson calls this type the "man-woman" —its counterpart should be characters like Richard Bumpus, in *Pastors and Masters*, and Felix Bacon, in *More Women Than Men*, who are small, dark, homosexual, intelligent, good characters: they also are adept at saving people's faces.

The aloof male character is usually aloof because of an absorbing intellectual interest. Almeric Bode, in *A House and Its Head*, "had attained the stage in letters, of honest despair of contemporary work"—that is far for a young man of twenty-six to have attained by Christmas Day in the year eighteen eighty-five, unaided as he might have been fifty or sixty years later by Cambridge criticism, but it is only a negative attainment; it is not enough to hold him. Later he loses his aloofness and elopes with Alison Edgeworth (it is fair to him to say that it must have been her idea).

The real, aloof, neuter, male character has more solid attainments and enjoys the companionship of a sister far superior to Dulcia Bode. Such is Stephen Marcon, in *Daughters and Sons*, a scientist who "had chosen medicine as the nearest to his own line, viewing its practical side with deprecation, its human contacts with distaste, its system of fees as displeasing and unfit . . . an obscure country doctor, with his science the pursuit of his leisure, which was the greater part of his life." Such another is Lester Marlowe, who has been content to spend two years on writing a book that brought him in sixty pounds—and from what we know of him we can imagine that it was a good book and that he was rightly content. Another such character is Olton Scrope in *The Present and the Past*.

The aloof woman is sometimes less kindly dealt with. "Miss Seymour [also in *Daughters and Sons*] was generally addressed as Jane, and did not dislike the custom, as she had an inability to be intimate with anyone, and felt it was disguised by an appearance of intimacy with everyone"—even as the present age of universal Christian names is an age in which intimacy is a rare thing. Jane talks about her own "personality", a thing in which she is totally lacking: in this she is like Clara Bell, in *Elders and Betters* ("known as Claribel to the family, and to as many people outside it as she could contrive"), who also speaks of the personality she lacks. They are the most characterless of all this author's characters—possessing, however, enough "character" to be clearly distinguished one from the other—which is not because they are unsuccessfully drawn but because it is their character to be without character.

### (6) *The Lower Orders*

Among these, it is only the underlings who are victimized: the upper servants, who are tyrants over them, are careful to have a very easy life.

Bethia (Edgeworth) is next in the house to Duncan Edgeworth himself; a kind of judge in Israel, Deborah to his Jehovah. Jennet (Chace), the other head parlour-maid, is a more downright and less alarming character—she is less characterized, for an important "messenger's speech" will be put into her mouth, and perhaps her personality might distract us if it were more emphatic.

The Haslams' Buttermere despises them as a *parvenu* family
and hopes (no doubt) that it will be his function to be present
as Fury or Fate at a very sensational debacle—and indeed it
would be no common experience to wait at breakfast on the
family half-an-hour or so after the eldest son had been hanged
for matricide. His disappointment deserves some sympathy
and gets it from Rachel Hardisty: "Think of being balked of
what you would like best in the world, when in sight of
it."

The Gavestons' Jellamy is also a brooding figure—at least
he seems so to his mistress, who orders him out of the room
whenever she has the chance.

The Clares' Ainger may seem to the reader uncomfortably
reminiscent at times of P. G. Wodehouse (a suspicion that
other of the author's menservants have sometimes aroused);
it is possible, however, that both authors are true to a kind of
life which the reader, in later and more uncomfortable days,
can no longer distinctly remember.

The servants are perhaps best in dialogue, in their choric
laments for death or approaching death, where they combine
the ghoulishness of their class with their function as part of a
Greek chorus.

"Poor Miss Donne will never take a cup of tea again," said
Cook (in *Elders and Betters*).

"That is what it means; death," said Cook.

And, in *Manservant and Maidservant*, the butler and the cook
enjoy Horace Lamb's funeral in anticipation:

" 'The hour is at hand. There will be the sad word to pass,
and the sad function will supervene.'

" 'As I had not overlooked. But I suppose instructions will be forthcoming.'

" 'And through my lips, Mrs Selden, and perhaps the moment is hardly premature. The males of the household will attend, that is to say myself, Mr. Mortimer and George, in our respective place. The other sex will remain under this roof, but I put in a plea for yourself, as moving on a different plane, and it is accepted that you will be present.'

" 'Well, plea is rather a strange term for a suggestion of such a nature,' said Cook on a rising tone. 'But there are differences that cannot be passed over, as you imply. So I will not refuse to lift my voice, even though the occasion may pierce the heart.'

" 'And have you mourning of a suitable character happening to lie by you?' said Bullivant, on his musical note.

" 'I am in a position to appear in black from head to foot,' said Cook, with a touch of aloofness . . . 'I suppose the master will be borne by his tenants to his grave?'

" 'That will be the course, Mrs Selden.'

" 'I hope to be equal to my part,' said Cook, bringing to Bullivant a vision of her, abandoned to song, while other voices swelled in her support.

" 'We shall follow the master in our time,' he said, 'though we know not on what day nor at what hour.'

" 'I do not ask to see,' said Cook, 'the distant scene. One step is enough for me.' "

Among the lower orders are also to be found two extra-ordinary characters, either of whom would alone make the fortune of a novel. In *Manservant and Maidservant* there is Miss

Buchanan of the village shop, who cannot read and spends her life in covering up this deficiency—and in *Parents and Children* is Mullet, the splendid, Dickensian nursery-maid, who entertains the Sullivan children with stories of her early splendour.

# CHAPTER 6

## *The Writing*

---

### (1) *Summary*

FEW AUTHORS HAVE used less summary, have made fewer comments on their people and happenings, have more completely excluded their own personalities from their work.

A minimum of summary there must be, in any work that is read and not acted. The scene is set in a few bare words. "It might be better", the author admits in the *Conversation* (a grudging admission, on which she had fortunately not bothered to act) "to give more account of people's homes and intimate background, but I hardly see why the date and style of the Gavestons' house should be given, as I did not think of them as giving their attention to it, and as a house of different date and style would have done for them equally well. It would be something to them that it was old and beautiful, but it would be enough."

It has to have been the family home for some generations, to be dilapidated and worthy of the restoration that it needs— and Matty, in her small house, must be able to regard her connection with the great house with complacent envy. But the upkeep of the great house must be a burden on the family and it must seem an enemy to Clement Gaveston. These requirements could as well be fulfilled by a Jacobean, William-and-Mary, or Palladian country house: there has therefore been no need to tell us which it was.

In *Brothers and Sisters* the village of Moreton Edge is named

—this is an exception. It is near enough to London for one to go back and forth in a day; and from the village in *Daughters and Sons* Charity Marcon can go up to London for a day at the British Museum. Otherwise we do not need to know where these villages are, and this author tells us nothing that we do not need to know. Who can say if the "prosperous English town" where Josephine Napier has her school is on the sea or no?

"As regards landscape and scenery", the author has said, "I never feel inclined to describe them; indeed I tend to miss such writing out, when I am reading . . ." The only exception is the attempted suicide of George: "He looked at the sky and the shadowy slopes, and drank in their beauty for the last time, without any idea that it was also the first."

The characters have always been "described enough to help people to imagine them", though often in terse phrases that do not remain in the memory. On going back, to compare and contrast characters that have seemed alike in other ways, one will sometimes find them physically alike—as we found Emily Herrick like Juliet Cassidy, Richard Bumpus like Felix Bacon, Jane Seymour like Clara Bell and Mr Merry like Mr Bode; other such likenesses could be collected (e.g. Mrs Blackwood, in *Dolores*, is like Mrs Christy). Perhaps the physical likeness may be due to the fact that some of these pairs derive (in some measure) from the same prototype in "real life"—Dickens, we know, made Mr Micawber and Old Dorrit with the use of the same model, his father. Perhaps the author associates, for other reasons, certain physical with certain spiritual qualities.

Now and then these descriptions are strikingly beautiful. This, for example: "Miss Charity Marcon walked up her garden path, crossed her hall and entered her plain little drawing-room, her great height almost coinciding with the door, and her long neck bending, lest the experience of years should prove at fault and it should quite coincide with it." In view of such a passage from *Daughters and Sons*, it is hard to agree with Miss Hansford-Johnson that the later books are more *seeable*.

Narrative, when it is not reported in a "messenger's speech", tends to be brief, epigrammatic and antithetical—its main purpose, apart from description, is to indicate the passage of time:

"The midday meal was not on the table, the first sign that Hetta was not in the house. The servants were so used to waiting for orders, that they had waited, giving themselves to their emotions. The young people almost wondered if such things would be held to count. But John gave a calm, firm order for the meal, the first sign that others would do what his sister had done. Sabine hardly ate and hardly stayed at the table, and resumed her wanderings, now with a low wail. . . .

"The day seemed to get itself to its end. Hetta was not there to guide it. The hours could only pass by themselves, dragging, failing, breaking down. The evening meal was on the table. It was met by a feeling of surprise and dim relief. Things could happen without Hetta. Other people could do what she had done; other people did what she had taught them to do."

In another passage, time passes very simply and barely, but

there is an undertone of faintly sinister suggestion: "Clement remained at the window after his brother had left him. He was to stand there several times in the next two months. At the end of them he came to the room where his sister was alone."

## (2) *The Stage-directions*

Only Henry James ever gave such minute directions for the performance of his dialogue.

The people may speak "consideringly, cordially, drily, earnestly, easily, frankly, gravely, grimly, judicially, leniently, miserably, playfully, quietly, almost brightly, almost pleasantly, almost tenderly, rather hurriedly" and "rather uneasily", with an air of "mild surprise, apology, enjoyment, amused admission" or "grave distaste".

They speak in "resigned acceptance, full admission, questioning agreement, incredulous appreciation, a guilty" or "a low aghast aside, almost excited assurance, a sort of burst, some consternation, open exasperation, bustling explanation, a light parenthesis, grave" or "rallying reproach, instant and almost harsh reproof, a complimentary but indefinite" or "a lightened" or "a suspicious but still incurious spirit" and "apparent unconsciousness".

A character may speak: "admitting more feeling than she knew into the last word; almost with archness, indifference, on a shriek; as if at the end of his endurance; as if voicing a mechanical thought; as though putting her observation in a more acceptable form; on a desperate impulse; half laughing; his eyes taking a covert general survey; his lips just framing the words; just articulating his words; just raising her brows; leaning forward earnestly; looking round frigidly; nodding his head up and down; striving for a natural manner; stumbling over the words; suddenly seeming to thrust out her words; trying to speak lightly; yielding to the situation".

The manner of a character may be: "absent, arch, automatic, detached, dubious, frank, glowing, harsh, hearty, jerky, neutral, offhand, parenthetic, pleasant, preoccupied, repressive, restless, rhythmic, ruminative, soothing, surprised, almost obliging (severe, stricken), rather quizzical, somewhat explosive, unusually unsparing, hushed and rueful, light and lively, even but somehow ruthless, conventional and therefore unnatural".

A character may speak with "peaceful lips, his careful laugh, a faint smile, a conscious smile, heaving shoulders, doubtful laughter, a good-natured chuckle, a roguish eye, a little sound of mirth, full enjoyment" or "a kind of charged brightness", with "conscious slowness and sadness, tears in her voice, tears under his words, a sort of groan, sighing resignation, almost fervent hopelessness; simple emphasis, reassurance, sincerity, straightforwardness, terseness, testiness, understanding; amused confidence, briskness and truth, cold carelessness, deliberate dryness, full and womanly concession, grave gallantry, indulgent fluency, mingled firmness and sympathy, nonchalant coldness, obvious reluctance, quiet understanding, rueful frankness, sudden concern, unusual gravity, weary shrewdness", with a touch of "abandon in her gait, apprehension, archness, excitement, firmness, grimness, heat, indignation, rough kindliness, sympathy, violence".

The tone in which a character speaks may be "acquiescent, aloof, astonished, audible, automatic, baffled, breathless, bewildered, careless, comfortable, consoling, deep, downright, drawling, driven, easy, even, frank, faltering, gentle, grave, judicial, low, lifeless, mellow, modest, musing, nonchalant, practical, quavering, reproachful, smothered, tentative, unprejudiced, wondering, zestful". It may be almost "businesslike, engaging, rallying, shouting, stricken, taunting, troubled". It may be "sudden, piercing; quiet, charged; incidental, cordial; tender, almost shaken; coaxing, deprecating; vaguely reproachful; faintly recitative", a tone of "appreciation, calm after storm, compunction, congratulation, returning hope, simple meekness, receiving light, stricken rejoinder, self-abasement, final and hopeless reiteration".

The voice may be "almost regretful; beautiful, self-conscious; choked; clear, carrying; clear, slow, almost ruthless; deep, vibrating; deep, dragging; rather empty; faint; harsh, stumbling; high, stammering, strong; high, rather insistent; low, almost crooning; intoning; sibilant, incisive; normal, gentle; rapid, breathless; sonorous; shrill, anxious; soft, staccato".

They may speak on a note of "avoiding perfunctoriness; comfort; despair; excuse; patience under provocation; propitiation; triumphant pride", or on a note that is "almost retaliatory; faintly corrective, reckless; scolding; piercing; unsparing; wary; wistful".

Here are about two hundred and fifty of the different ways in which the characters may speak, and there may be nearly as many ways more; the author can thus give a very great precision to her effects of dialogue.

The sibilant hiss and the drawl of tyranny are particularly blood-curdling—James Harlowe, Clarissa's hateful brother, drawled in the same way. On the whole, though the stage directions modify the utterances of all the characters, it is the bad or dishonest characters who most call them into use, for the good people's words are more able to speak for themselves.

## (3) *The Dialogue*

The story is mainly told, and the characters are entirely revealed, by dialogue—a dialogue of incomparable brilliance, bright, glittering, too clever (so they say) for some readers. The words that best give a general description of it are those once used by Thomas de Quincey to describe Southey's style: "a trenchant, pungent, aculeated form of terse, glittering, stenographic sentences."

"I thought", writes Mr Somerset Maugham of one of his early books "that . . . I would try to make my characters speak not the words they would actually have spoken, but in a more formal manner, using the phrases they would have used if they had been able to prepare them beforehand and had known how to put what they wanted to say in exact and well-chosen language."

This is not Miss Compton-Burnett's formula, though it would cover some of the speeches—sometimes the utterances of characters are nearer to or identical with those of "real life".

There are simple characters, people of few words, whether adults or children, whose speech is not stylized.

" 'How do you do, Mrs Napier? I have come back to-day because the term begins to-morrow.'

"Having uttered this greeting, Miss Emmeline Munday stood at ease and in silence."

These were generally her portion; Muriel Ponsonby, a child

of eleven, had a harder lot than a senior English mistress and was seldom at ease, though usually silent.

"You do not—you need not—Miss Bunyan—you need not eat more than you want at tea." Muriel's words are perfectly natural.

The language is not always exact and well-chosen; Josephine Napier is sometimes allowed to use slang, and so is Dulcia Bode.

"A nice kind of customer," says Josephine. Again, she says: "There would be a fine to-do, if I did. I am not courting such a shindy." And she speaks of "my experienced phiz".

Josephine's use of slang, not very natural in a headmistress aged fifty-four, is part of her insincerity; it is also (perhaps) in part a result of her claims on the masculine world—she is vain of having more to do with it than the other women in the book.

Dulcia's slang: "I am a prize ass! . . . I am a drivelling idiot!" are part of her exhibitionism and the pride that she can see a joke against herself.

Dulcia, we have already seen, has a tendency to cliché; she really feels, or persuades herself that she feels, as journalists say they feel.

She has, as all users of abundant cliché must have, a marked tendency to mixed metaphor. "You plucked up your courage, and faced the music. That was not square dealing. . . . I have screwed my courage to the pitch. Turn and rend me if you must; I am going to take the plunge . . . I'll go bail he will not raise Cain: I undertake to square him. . . . That hits the nail! That strikes the wavering balance!" Her feelings about the Edgeworths are very much the same as those that journalists express about the royal family.

She is awkward with downright, sincere people, such as Gretchen or Cassandra Jekyll or Florence Smollett, and really seems to feel her inferiority to them (though at times she may think she is their superior in sensitiveness or seriousness). When she tries to talk like them, the result is embarrassing: "I am going to talk in an ordinary way," she says to Cassandra, after her mother's death. "Something tells me you would prefer that vehicle of sympathy." Moreover she is very careful to talk about sex in a frank and natural way, behind which the effort is felt.

Sophia has also a tendency to cliché, as perhaps everyone must have who makes the most of the drama of life and meets big occasions with big speeches: "We will turn our faces to the future, and live in the present, and let the dead past bury its dead. If we ever know more of the truth, we will meet it with a strong front."

The more obvious faults of speech—the italics of Mr Blackwood, the boring anecdotage of Dr Cassell, the break in the middle of words affected by Mrs Merton-Vane (all in *Dolores*) are weaknesses of early work, never permitted in the novels of her maturity. Not for her the easy device of the stammer, with which less gifted writers of dialogue have to be content; she has far more fundamental ways of showing who is speaking.

But some of her discoveries, which date back as far as this early book, have rightly been thought worthy of revival. Mr Blackwood's "out-and-out awful thing" recurs in *Brothers and Sisters* as Cousin Peter's "out-and-out suitable thing" or his "out-and-out horrible thing", and his pompous "I can tell you that it does" is echoed in Cousin Peter's "I can say she will". And the diffidence of Soulsby: "She—I suppose—what will she do while you are working?" is revived in Edgar Gaveston: "We are certainly more useful—have more chance of being of use when we are not tired out."

That some of her characters should know how to put what they want to say in exact and well-chosen language is far from unnatural: many of the characters are by nature clever and witty—such as Emily Herrick, Julian Wake, Rachel Hardisty, Francis Bacon, Grant Edgeworth, Evelyn Seymour, Hope Cranmer, Bernard Donne, Mortimer Lamb, Gaunt Lovat—the list is by no means exhaustive. There is a number of professional writers among the characters who must have training in words: Nicholas Herrick, Charity Marcon, John and France Ponsonby, not to speak of unpublished amateurs like the young Staces, and Jonathan Swift, who waits for the verdict of posterity. The numbers of members of the scholastic profession are very large, governesses, schoolmasters and mistresses, university lecturers; there are also clergymen who must be accustomed to public speaking.

Moreover, some of the less articulate, children or lower servants, are trying to learn to talk and they pay heed to their language; the upper servants, with every justification, take pride in their powers of self-expression. The Edgeworths' Bethia "was always one for expressions", and the Sullivans' Hatton was considered by her nursery-maid Mullet (herself a wonderful raconteuse) "as pointed and finished as any lady".

Nor should we forget that the action of the books takes place before the horrible destruction that two wars have made in the quality of spoken English. Therefore, while we must still call much of the dialogue stylized, it is not so much stylized as many people seem to think.

Nevertheless stylization is there and, like any language that is at all remote from living speech, that of Miss Compton-Burnett does not escape occasional clumsiness and woodenness. It is too exact a transcription of thought, while speech is both more and less than that.

"It is the intangibility of the distinction that gives it its point," says Lucia Sullivan.

Too often characters will express thought with the precision of philosophers and will answer one another's thoughts rather than one another's words. It does not matter if the resulting dialogue is too stenographic for the lazy reader—the author is not writing for the lazy and the inattentive—but the discerning reader, who understands, cannot always admire. Nor can the grace of euphony be sacrificed quite with impunity. When I first met Miss Compton-Burnett's work, in *A House and Its Head*, I wondered uneasily for some pages whether she could write at all before I discovered that she wrote better than any living novelist: many readers must experience the same bewilderment. This bewilderment should be overcome, but it is not a virtue of the writer's style that, on a first approach, it should give rise to it.

Mr Somerset Maugham's formula will not take us very far —for the author is uncannily adept at making the characters give themselves away in one way or another. We see every degree of insincerity: the totally untrue scene worked up by Anna Donne to conceal her deception about Sukey's will is the extreme of lying. The "forgeries of jealousy" of Sophia Hutton, Josephine Napier and Hetta Ponsonby are falsehoods in which the possessive women would themselves like to believe, and it is likely that they convince themselves rather more than their hearers. Josephine tries to make out that she and Gabriel are rather aloof from his marriage and not much interested: "But do not breathe a whisper, and you shall see that we shall not betray ourselves." Hetta pretends that she arranged a second marriage for her brother John: "Mind you don't betray me. I think John is really attached to her."

There is the conscientious irony of those two excellent women, Miss Burtenshaw and Miss Fellowes, when Mr Jekyll is lost to them by marriage with Nance Edgeworth; they are touching and dignified and careful not to tell lies, though they hide their feelings—Newman might have held them up as an example of virtuous dissimulation. With them in mind, we are able to condemn Hetta and Josephine.

There is the more trivial lying of the exhibitionists, snobs, prigs and toadies. The degree of insincerity probably differs in each character: thus Dominic Spong, who is aware of (and wholly tolerant of) his own smarminess, is a less abandoned character than Dr Chaucer, whose vice is the lie in the soul— it is right that Dominic Spong should marry Camilla, while Chaucer is condemned to marriage with Hetta Ponsonby.

Although Anna Donne gets away with the largest and flattest of lies, lying is dangerous—you may win money by it but if what you want is the love and confidence of one of the good characters, you are likely to lose it. It was because of her lies that Agatha Calkin lost Gregory Haslam and she did not even know that they were lies. And, by a meanness being discovered, Magdalen Doubleday lost Mortimer Lamb.

" 'You must trust me,' said Magdalen.

" 'But that is what I cannot do. At any time you might act for my good. When people do that, it kills something precious between them.' "

Another formula can be found in these words from Miss M. C. Bradbrooke's book, *Themes and Conventions of Elizabethan Tragedy*. "Sometimes the *dramatis personae* exchange speeches in the modern manner, where each character has his limited role and remains inside it: sometimes the character, still inside his role, will approach the spectators; sometimes again a character may transcend the limits of his special role and assume a kind of choric speech, in which he states the total situation and expresses the 'moral' or central significance of the play."

Perhaps I may put beside this two passages of my own, describing Miss Compton-Burnett's dialogue, either of which would be applicable to Elizabethan drama.

"Its nearness to or remoteness from ordinary spoken language will vary from place to place. There is no single formula that will cover it." And: "Her idiom sometimes approximates to what one might actually say if one were in the character's skin and situation, but also to what one might think of saying and bite back; to what one might afterwards wish one had said; to what one would like other people to think; and to what one would like to think oneself. It is unlikely that these alternatives are exclusive."[1]

It is absurd to say (in view of all the forms of insincerity that are explored) that the characters "speak precisely as they are thinking." The most general formula that can be offered is that the dominant need of the character usually speaks—this may be inward-looking or outward-looking, concerned with what he thinks or with appearances, and therefore he may speak truth or lies.

As for speeches that in real life we would bite back, many of the characters are particularly characterized by boldness

[1] *A Treatise on the Novel.*

in speech, and go very much further than most of us would.

" 'I do not feel I could bite my tongue out,' murmured Grant Edgeworth."

" 'You observe that my sisters are outspoken, Miss Hallam, where a normal self-respect would keep them silent,' said Victor Ponsonby."

Sir Rowland Seymour says about the Ponsonbys: "What I can't understand about that family, is how they say what they like all the time, and yet seem to be frightened. Can anyone explain it?"

This is, I think, a warning that we are not to take too many of the speeches as being silent thoughts. "People do not know about families". "The venomous words, the insults that never cease to rankle, the invisible thrusts of the stiletto, the infernal second intentions in speech, for that matter the mere irreparable slips of the tongue . . ." Greatly driven, the young will answer back sometimes—it does not pay, but there is an awful satisfaction in drawing blood, and they are supported by the love and courage of their allies. Moreover, a good many speeches are made *sotto voce* to an ally but are overheard—Duncan Edgeworth is not the only tyrant whose hearing is erratic; one never knows how much he will hear and how much he will not; and ubiquity has been a characteristic of female tyrants from Sophia Stace onwards—they may at any moment appear in any part of the house. It is certainly a characteristic of the female tyrant in "real life".

"I wonder if we have prompted things as often as we think

we have," said Josephine, almost in soliloquy. She was speaking for an audience, Godfrey Haslam's soliloquies are not for an audience and almost approach an interior monologue: "Well, my Gregory and Polly! Well, my pretty pair! I can tell you I envy you; or I should in some people's place. I know what you are feeling. It only comes once, at whatever time of life it comes, what is carrying you on its force. Some people would say you were too young, as they would say that I was too old. They are as wrong in one case as in the other. For we know not on what day nor in what hour it cometh, whether in the spring or the autumn, the later summer of life."

There are the speeches that are half meant to be heard:

" 'We have hushed enough things up,' said Nance under her breath."

" 'We are untrained certainly: that has been attended to,' said Victor in an undertone half meant to be heard."

In the later books there are speeches that we are told are silent:

" 'My dear, think what you are saying. What makes you talk like that?' says someone (probably Justine Gaveston) to Aubrey—that lovely character, whose utterances are sometimes like those of the fool in *King Lear*, but who has been playing the fool.

" 'Excess of feeling and a wish to disguise it,' said Aubrey, but not aloud."

Terence Calderon, in *Elders and Betters*, is in some ways a more grown-up Aubrey. His is the next silent speech:

" 'I cannot claim to be anything but the typical, strung-up woman of the family [says Claribel, who is almost totally insensitive]. Birds of a feather flock together, and that must be my excuse for bringing more nerves and nervous emotions to a place where they exist in plenty.'
" 'There can be no excuse,' said Terence, in a voice that could almost be heard."

Two of the below-stairs characters in *Manservant and Maidservant* utter cries from the heart in silent speech. George is asked why he is stealing food.

" 'Because I am so plainly fed, that the dining-room pudding was irresistible,' said George, but only in his heart."

" 'If I were able to read, I should not have to be alone,' said Miss Buchanan, so nearly with her lips that her breath was quickened."

These silent speeches, definitely so described, make us

conjecture that many speeches, not specifically described as silent, may be unheard—I believe the author works within an almost Elizabethan convention, which gives her the liberty to pass at will from ordinary spoken dialogue to soliloquy heard only by the reader.

" 'Do take your hands out of your pockets, Robin,' said Sophia. 'I told you that just now. Can't you find something to occupy them? Or must you stand about all the evening because other people are in trouble?' [That is certainly ordinary, audible speech.]

" 'Yes, of course I must be about at people's service, when things are amiss, and they might have a use for me,' said Robin [and clearly this is speech of a very different sort and it may well be silent]. 'I hope you will do the same when you get down to Father. To do you justice, I believe you will. And I discover something to employ my hands in opening the door for you. You are doing harm up here.' "

Sophia gives no sign of having heard this speech, and very likely she could not.

Interior dialogue is also a thing that exists in life as well as in fiction: lovers who think that they can converse without words are often the victims of a pathetic fallacy, and many of us, no doubt, were conceived while our fathers were thinking of golf and our mothers of house-keeping or hats—but hatred can go deeper than love, and it is the tie of family, not of sex, that can cause such secret understanding. Flashes of venomous but unspoken wit can play dangerously over the breakfast table.

Any attempt at a schematic account, however, would bring us into error—we are to be poised, as in Greek or Shakespearian drama, ready to accept everyday speech, stichomythia, chorus, great tragic speeches, asides and soliloquies, and gnomic aphorisms. They all, miraculously, fit into the whole. "It is simply the result of an effort to give the impression I want to give."

Probably it was instinct rather than theory that so rightly guided the author to give us no background—the drama has been dead since the picture stage made chorus, soliloquy, aside, and great tragic speeches look self-conscious and absurd: the novel can, happily, dispense with a solid background.

## (4) *The Aphorisms*

These increase in number and brilliance with every book. Though often detachable and quotable, they are all imprinted with an individual mark—the thought and the rhythm reveal their author.

"To know all is to forgive all, and that would spoil everything."

"Being cruel to be kind is just ordinary cruelty with an excuse made for it. And it is right that it should be more resented, as it is."

"People are only human. But it really does not seem much for them to be."

"Saying a thing of yourself does not mean that you like to hear other people say it. And they do say it differently."

"I think it nearly always rains. We only notice it when it pours."

"Self-knowledge speaks ill for people; it shows they are what they are, almost on purpose."

"I feel that to know all is to forgive all, and other people seem to forgive nothing. And no one can say they don't know all. I have never thought of any way of keeping it from them."

"Of course we like to say that kind hearts are more than coronets, as if we met both."

"Familiarity breeds contempt, and ought to breed it. It is through familiarity that we get to know each other."

"Pride may go before a fall. But it may also continue after."

"Satisfied curiosity is the best thing in life. The only thing that is as good as it promises to be. Anticipation is not the best part of it."

" 'How we all like talking about ourselves!'
" 'And dislike it in other people. And of course they ought not to do it. Why should we want to know about them? As if it were as satisfying as knowing about us.' "

" 'You cannot eat your cake and have it.'

" 'That is a mean saying. You could, if you had enough cake. It is sad that it has become established. It throws a dark light on human nature.' "

"It is surprising how many people go where duty calls. I wonder if it is because they have nowhere else to go."

It is noticeable that many of these aphorisms result from the turning upside down of some conventional phrase or some piece of proverbial wisdom. Words that we often use unthinkingly to make do instead of thought are frequently and unsparingly exposed by her scrutiny.

Take this passage of dialogue from *Daughters and Sons*:

"Do you not advocate self-improvement in your profession?" the father asks the governess.

"I have never met it," she replies. "People are always improved by others. That is what gives rise to the profession."

"It is hard to see how the word, self-improvement, arose," says one of the daughters.

Or Elton Scrope, in *The Present and the Past*, on life:

" 'It is not short and will not soon be gone. It is longer than anyone can realize. And it is very brave to end it. To say it is cowardly is absurd. It is only said by people who would not dare to do it.' "

Or Bridget, in *Darkness and Day*, on time:

" 'Time has too much credit. . . . It is not a great healer. It is an indifferent and perfunctory one. Sometimes it does not heal at all. And sometimes when it seems to, no healing has been necessary.' "

Or Juliet, in *Two Worlds and their Ways*:

" 'You are clutching at a straw. And when people do that, it does sometimes save them.' "

Or Oliver, in the same book:

" 'I do not shrink from self-praise. It is so untrue that it is no recommendation.' "

## (5) *The Stichomythia*

Not only do the happenings of Greek tragedy occur in these novels, but also some of its methods—*stichomythia*, the rapid interchange of one-line or of very short speeches has never been so much acclimatized in English before. Miss Compton-Burnett is free to multiply speakers, as the Greek tragedians were not, but some of her best effects are in duologue:

" 'Sibyl is very much affected by the shock,' said Dulcia, as they went home. 'I could not have believed it would take her as it has. I am not at liberty to divulge the truth, but no one would believe it who had not her confidence.'

" 'I suppose it is natural.'

" 'It is not natural. It is morbid and strange. As I said, I should not have believed it.'

" 'I should, you know,' said Beatrice, in a frank tone. 'I saw she was overwrought, in all the ways that do not go into words.'

" 'You have no suspicion, happily for your peace. And it did go into words, unhappily for mine.'

" 'I have not much peace on her account, I confess.'

" 'You would have none, if you knew.'

" 'I do not know specifically, of course; but I have a shrewd suspicion.'

" 'No, dear; your suspicions may be shrewd; but you are not on the nail here. No. And I am glad you are not.'

" 'Can I help you in the place you are in?'

" 'No, I am not going to reveal it. I must be strong. I must not be led into betraying a trust, by such insinuating offers.' "

This is a comic passage, but this and other passages suggest a method of rendering Greek *stichomythia* more satisfactory than any that has yet been tried.

The confession of Phaedra from the *Hippolytus* of Euripides will do as an example: I take the liberty of inserting "stage-directions".

" 'Has Theseus wronged you in any of the ways that do not go into words?' said the Nurse.

" 'I hope I shall not be seen as having behaved badly to-wards him,' said Phaedra.

" 'What then is it?' said the Nurse, in a coaxing, cajoling tone. 'This terrible thing that arouses your wish to die?'

" 'Let me do wrong,' said Phaedra, on a reckless note. 'I do not do you wrong.'

" 'I suppose you think I like losing you?' said the Nurse, with a little burst of bitter mirth. 'I suppose you think just that.'

" 'Oh, what are you about?' said Phaedra. 'Are you holding on to my arms to force me?'

" 'And I will hold your knees too, and I will not be put off.'

" 'It will be a very bad thing for you, poor Nurse,' said Phaedra. 'A very bad thing for you, if you find it out.'

" 'Can anything be so bad for me as to be without you?' said the Nurse.

.      .      .      .      .

" 'Oh!' said Phaedra. 'Can you not put into words for me, what I have to say?'

" 'I am not a fortune-teller,' said the Nurse. 'I cannot know what is hidden.'

" 'What do people mean,' said Phaedra, 'when they say someone is in love?'

" 'It is something very sweet, my dear,' said the Nurse. 'And it is very bitter at the same time.'

" 'It is only the second part that has been my portion,' said Phaedra.

" 'What are you saying, child?' said the Nurse. 'Who is the man?'

" 'Whoever he is, the Amazon's son,' said Phaedra, covering her mouth with her hand.

" 'Do you mean Hippolytus?'

" 'You spoke his name, not I,' said Phaedra, in choked tones."

## (6) *The Great Tragic Speeches*

Of these she has always been a mistress, ever since the great last scene between Matthew and his mother in *Men and Wives*. A tendency to verse, perhaps not altogether intended, perhaps given more attention than it should be by an ear accustomed to some of Mr Eliot's later rhythms, seems to mark some of the later books.

Sir Roderick Shelley says:

"It is the hidden thing that does not flourish.
Nothing can grow without the light.
We can only tend it as we can, leaving it safe in the dark.
And although 'out of sight' may not mean 'out of mind',
This talk must be as if it had not been.
We must trust each other."

There is a great scene between Edmund and Bridget in *Darkness and Day* which is also, perhaps, best read as verse.

EDMUND: We cannot use light words, but we could use none.
But you have overborne me.
When you say that your weakness bears me down, you say the truth.
You are too weak to face your weakness,
And there is no truer strength.
You will say what you must, shed your own light, bring your own darkness.

And I shall stand by you, making your will mine.
I have no will of my own.

BRIDGET: We are fluent, Edmund. We have said it before.
We seem to be acting a scene. And that is what we are doing.
But it will not help us when the time comes.
The scene will rise out of the moment, as scenes do.
I can feel your mother's eyes on me, my own eyes falling before
    them.
These rehearsals will not stand us in any stead.

# Bibliography

Dolores, 1911

Pastors and Masters, 1925

Brothers and Sisters, 1929

Men and Wives, 1931

More Women Than Men, 1933

A House and Its Head, 1935

Daughters and Sons, 1937

A Family and A Fortune, 1939

Parents and Children, 1941

Elders and Betters, 1944

A Conversation between I. Compton-Burnett and M. Jourdain
(in *Orion: a Miscellany*), 1945

Manservant and Maidservant, 1947

Two Worlds and Their Ways, 1949

Darkness and Day, 1951

The Present and the Past, 1953

Mother and Son (to be published in 1955)